Manhattan Review™

Test Prep & Admissions Consulting

Turbocharge Your SAT: Critical Reading Guide

part of the 2nd Edition Series

April 20th, 2016

- ☐ *Designed as per the revised SAT*
- ☐ *Complete & challenging training sets: 12 passages; 130 questions*
- ☐ *Never-seen-before dedicated "Understanding the passage" section*
- ☐ *Visually-appealing section: "Reading through creating impressions"*
- ☐ *Concept illustration through graphic aids and info-graphic strips*
- ☐ *10 proven SAT-reading strategies*
- ☐ *Ample "Reasoning-based" questions*
- ☐ *Ample newly-introduced "Graphics & Calculation-based" questions 8 graphs; 16 questions*

www.manhattanreview.com

Copyright and Terms of Use

Copyright and Trademark

All materials herein (including names, terms, trademarks, designs, images, and graphics) are the property of Manhattan Review, except where otherwise noted. Except as permitted herein, no such material may be copied, reproduced, displayed or transmitted or otherwise used without the prior written permission of Manhattan Review. You are permitted to use material herein for your personal, noncommercial use, provided that you do not combine such material into a combination, collection, or compilation of material. If you have any questions regarding the use of the material, please contact Manhattan Review at info@manhattanreview.com.

This material may make reference to countries and persons. The use of such references is for hypothetical and demonstrative purposes only.

Terms of Use

By using this material, you acknowledge and agree to the terms of use contained herein.

No Warranties

This material is provided without warranty, either express or implied, including the implied warranties of merchantability, of fitness for a particular purpose and noninfringement. Manhattan Review does not warrant or make any representations regarding the use, accuracy or results of the use of this material. This material may make reference to other source materials. Manhattan Review is not responsible in any respect for the content of such other source materials, and disclaims all warranties and liabilities with respect to the other source materials.

Limitation on Liability

Manhattan Review shall not be responsible under any circumstances for any direct, indirect, special, punitive, or consequential damages ("Damages") that may arise from the use of this material. In addition, Manhattan Review does not guarantee the accuracy or completeness of its course materials, which are provided "as is" with no warranty, express or implied. Manhattan Review assumes no liability for any Damages from errors or omissions in the material, whether arising in contract, tort or otherwise.

SAT is a registered trademark of the College Board.
College Board does not endorse, nor is it affiliated in any way with, the owner of this product or any content herein.

10-Digit International Standard Book Number: (ISBN: 1-62926-098-3)
13-Digit International Standard Book Number: (ISBN: 978-1-62926-098-3)

Last updated on April 20th, 2016.

Manhattan Review, 275 Madison Avenue, Suite 1429, New York, NY 10016.
Phone: +1 (212) 316-2000. E-Mail: info@manhattanreview.com. Web: www.manhattanreview.com

About the Turbocharge your SAT Series

The Turbocharge Your SAT Series was created to provide students with comprehensive and highly effective SAT preparation for maximum SAT performance. Thousands of students around the world have received substantial score improvements by using Manhattan Review's SAT prep books. Now in its updated 2nd edition for the new SAT in 2016, the full series of 12 guides is designed to provide SAT students with rigorous, thorough, and accessible SAT instruction for top SAT scores. Manhattan Review's SAT prep books precisely target each testing area and deconstruct the different test sections in a manner that is both student-centered and results-driven, teaching test-takers everything they need to know in order to significantly boost their scores. Covering all of the necessary material in mathematics and verbal skills from the most basic through the most advanced levels, the Turbocharge Your SAT Series is the top study resource for all stages of SAT preparation. Students who work through the complete series develop all of the skills, knowledge, and strategies needed for their best possible SAT scores.

- ☐ SAT Math Essentials (ISBN: 978-1-62926-090-7)
- ☐ SAT Arithmetic Guide (ISBN: 978-1-62926-091-4)
- ☐ SAT Algebra Guide (ISBN: 978-1-62926-092-1)
- ☐ SAT Geometry Guide (ISBN: 978-1-62926-093-8)
- ☐ SAT Permutation, Combination & Probability Guide (ISBN: 978-1-62926-094-5)
- ☐ SAT Statistics & Data Analysis Guide (ISBN: 978-1-62926-095-2)
- ☐ SAT Trigonometry & Complex Numbers Guide (ISBN: 978-1-62926-096-9)
- ☐ SAT Quantitative Question Bank (ISBN: 978-1-62926-097-6)
- ☐ SAT Sentence Correction Guide (ISBN: 978-1-62926-067-9)
- ■ SAT Critical Reading Guide (ISBN: 978-1-62926-098-3)
- ☐ SAT Reading Comprehension Guide (ISBN: 978-1-62926-069-3)
- ☐ SAT Writing & Language Test Guide (ISBN: 978-1-62926-099-0)
- ☐ SAT Essay Guide (ISBN: 978-1-62926-100-3)
- ☐ SAT Vocabulary Builder (ISBN: 978-1-62926-101-0)

About the Company

Manhattan Review's origin can be traced directly back to an Ivy League MBA classroom in 1999. While teaching advanced quantitative subjects to MBAs at Columbia Business School in New York City, Professor Dr. Joern Meissner developed a reputation for explaining complicated concepts in an understandable way. Prof. Meissner's students challenged him to assist their friends, who were frustrated with conventional test preparation options. In response, Prof. Meissner created original lectures that focused on presenting standardized test content in a simplified and intelligible manner, a method vastly different from the voluminous memorization and so-called tricks commonly offered by others. The new methodology immediately proved highly popular with students, inspiring the birth of Manhattan Review.

Since its founding, Manhattan Review has grown into a multi-national educational services firm, focusing on preparation for the major undergraduate and graduate admissions tests, college admissions consulting, and application advisory services, with thousands of highly satisfied students all over the world. Our SAT instruction is continuously expanded and updated by the Manhattan Review team, an enthusiastic group of master SAT professionals and senior academics. Our team ensures that Manhattan Review offers the most time-efficient and cost-effective preparation available for the SAT. Please visit www.ManhattanReview.com for further details.

About the Founder

Professor Dr. Joern Meissner has more than 25 years of teaching experience at the graduate and undergraduate levels. He is the founder of Manhattan Review, a worldwide leader in test prep services, and he created the original lectures for its first test preparation classes. Prof. Meissner is a graduate of Columbia Business School in New York City, where he received a PhD in Management Science. He has since served on the faculties of prestigious business schools in the United Kingdom and Germany. He is a recognized authority in the areas of supply chain management, logistics, and pricing strategy. Prof. Meissner thoroughly enjoys his research, but he believes that grasping an idea is only half of the fun. Conveying knowledge to others is even more fulfilling. This philosophy was crucial to the establishment of Manhattan Review, and remains its most cherished principle.

International Phone Numbers and Official Manhattan Review Websites

Manhattan Headquarters	+1-212-316-2000	www.manhattanreview.com
USA & Canada	+1-800-246-4600	www.manhattanreview.com
Argentina	+1-212-316-2000	www.review.com.ar
Australia	+61-3-9001-6618	www.manhattanreview.com
Austria	+43-720-115-549	www.review.at
Belgium	+32-2-808-5163	www.manhattanreview.be
Brazil	+1-212-316-2000	www.manhattanreview.com.br
Chile	+1-212-316-2000	www.manhattanreview.cl
China	+86-20-2910-1913	www.manhattanreview.cn
Czech Republic	+1-212-316-2000	www.review.cz
France	+33-1-8488-4204	www.review.fr
Germany	+49-89-3803-8856	www.review.de
Greece	+1-212-316-2000	www.review.com.gr
Hong Kong	+852-5808-2704	www.review.hk
Hungary	+1-212-316-2000	www.review.co.hu
India	+1-212-316-2000	www.review.in
Indonesia	+1-212-316-2000	www.manhattanreview.id
Ireland	+1-212-316-2000	www.gmat.ie
Italy	+39-06-9338-7617	www.manhattanreview.it
Japan	+81-3-4589-5125	www.manhattanreview.jp
Malaysia	+1-212-316-2000	www.review.my
Netherlands	+31-20-808-4399	www.manhattanreview.nl
New Zealand	+1-212-316-2000	www.review.co.nz
Philippines	+1-212-316-2000	www.review.ph
Poland	+1-212-316-2000	www.review.pl
Portugal	+1-212-316-2000	www.review.pt
Qatar	+1-212-316-2000	www.review.qa
Russia	+1-212-316-2000	www.manhattanreview.ru
Singapore	+65-3158-2571	www.gmat.sg
South Africa	+1-212-316-2000	www.manhattanreview.co.za
South Korea	+1-212-316-2000	www.manhattanreview.kr
Sweden	+1-212-316-2000	www.gmat.se
Spain	+34-911-876-504	www.review.es
Switzerland	+41-435-080-991	www.review.ch
Taiwan	+1-212-316-2000	www.gmat.tw
Thailand	+66-6-0003-5529	www.manhattanreview.com
Turkey	+1-212-316-2000	www.review.com.tr
United Arab Emirates	+1-212-316-2000	www.manhattanreview.ae
United Kingdom	+44-20-7060-9800	www.manhattanreview.co.uk
Rest of the World	+1-212-316-2000	www.manhattanreview.com

Contents

Chapter 1

Welcome

Dear students,

Here at Manhattan Review, we constantly strive to provide you the best educational content for standardized test preparation. We make a tremendous effort to keep making things better and better for you. This is especially important with respect to an examination such as the SAT. As you know, in Spring 2016, the SAT underwent a major change. The revised SAT is challenging. The typical SAT aspirant is confused with so many test-prep options available. Your challenge is to choose a book or a tutor that prepares you for attaining your goal. We cannot say that we are one of the best; it is you who has to be the judge.

This book differs in many aspects from standard books available on the market. Unlike a book from any other prep company, this book discusses as many as 12 strategies in detail on how to approach SAT-Reading passages. We have discussed 12 SAT-like passages and approximately 130 questions. Each passage is explained in a never-seen-before dedicated section— Understanding the passages. We provide you with never-seen-before visually-appealing images to illustrate the concept of "Reading through creating impressions". While discussing options, we explain each option with why the correct option is right and why incorrect options are wrong. You will find plenty of questions on one of the rare categories—application or reasoning-based questions.

The revised SAT-Reading test is more challenging than before. The reading passages themselves may have graphs and associated questions. There will be at least a couple of graph based questions in the test, involving mathematical computations. Our book has as many as 8 graph-based passages, and 16 associated questions.

In a nut shell, Manhattan Review's "SAT-Reading" book is holistic and comprehensive in all respects; it is created so because we listen to what students need. Should you have any query, please feel free to write to us at info@manhattanreview.com.

Happy learning!

Professor Dr. Joern Meissner
& The Manhattan Review Team

Chapter 2

Introduction to the Revised SAT

The SAT has changed, with the revised SAT taking effect in the spring of 2016. The revised SAT will comprise two major sections: one, evidence-based reading & writing and two, math. The essay, which now is optional, is excluded from being a compulsory part of the SAT writing section. Evidence-based reading & writing has two sections: one, reading (only reading, no "critical" element is part of the title, but that does not mean that the new reading test will not test critical aspects of reading) and two, the writing & language test. This section has undergone a major change in its format. Questions testing your skills at writing, grammar, & language aspects will be taken from a passage. With both the reading & writing & language sections being passage-based, they may also include info-graphics within the passages, and there will be one or two questions based on a graph or a chart. There may be a hint of some math in the reading passages & the writing passages.

While the format of the math test remains unchanged, there are new additions in the math section. It will focus more on algebra and data analysis. You will see more questions on real-life situational charts and graphs in the test. There is an addition of two new topics: trigonometry & complex numbers. There will be one or two questions testing your higher order thinking. Those questions may be in a set of two questions, and will have a lengthy narration. Another special category of questions will be one in which you are asked to interpret a situation described mathematically in words; there will be four options, each being at least two lines, and only one of the options is correct. Another change to the math section is that there will be a section with no calculator allowed.

Two noticeable changes in the revised SAT are: one, there is no negative marking, and two, there are only four options in MCQs.

The following table shows a comparative analysis of the old SAT vs. the revised SAT.

The old SAT vs. the revised SAT

	Old SAT	Revised SAT
Sections	• Math • Critical Reading • Writing (incl. Essay)	• Math • Evidence-based reading & writing • Reading • Writing & language test • Essay (optional; exclusive of the writing & language test)
Content	• Reasoning skills • Contextual vocabulary • Applied mathematical problems	• Reasoning skills & knowledge of real-world situations • Evidence-based reading, writing, & math problems • Introduction of graphs & charts in passages, thereby testing associated questions (even calculation-based questions) • Contextual vocabulary in broader contexts • Introduction of trigonometry & complex numbers in math • Higher Order thinking questions in math
Question types	• Multiple Choice Questions (MCQ) • Student-produced response questions (Grid-In) in math	• Multiple Choice Questions (MCQ) • Student-produced response questions (Grid-In) in math

Number of options for MCQs	5 (A through E)	**4 (A through D)**
Negative marking	$-\frac{1}{4}$ for wrong answers	**No negative marking**
Scoring	<ul><li>Total score: 600–2400; incl. scores from Critical Reading, Writing, & Math (each score from 200–800)</li><li>Writing score includes essay score</li></ul>	<ul><li>Total score: 400–1600; incl. scores from evidence-based reading and writing, & math (each scored from 200–800)</li><li>Essays are scored separately (1–4)</li><li>Sub-scores & cross-scores (contribution from selected areas)</li></ul>
Timing	<ul><li>3 hours 45 minutes</li></ul>	<ul><li>3 hours (excluding essay)</li><li>3 hours 50 minutes (including essay)</li></ul>
Calculator access	Throughout the math section	There is a no-calculator section in the math section

Chapter 3

Introduction to SAT Reading test

 The SAT Reading Test consists entirely of Reading Comprehension (RC) tested with the help of passages and questions on those passages. While you may have come across RC in other tests, the ones you will see in the SAT will be unlike any others, but not as dull as you would find in higher-level standardized tests. The passages are drawn from a variety of sources to test your ability to comprehend verbal content across topics.

The SAT Reading Test is to be completed in 65 minutes, within which you have to answer a total of 52 questions from 4 individual passages and 1 set of paired passages. Each passage or set of paired passages will contain 500 to 750 words and have 10 or 11 questions. Questions will be of a variety of types, evaluating your general and specific understanding of the content. There will be four answer options per question.

•	Time	65 minutes
•	Questions	52
•	Single passages	4
•	Set of paired passages	1
•	Length of passage	500-750 words
•	Number of questions per passage	10-11
•	Number of options per question	4

Passage topics

The passage topics range from purely informational to reasoning-based. There will be one passage each on the topics of literature, history & social studies, and founding documents or great global conversation, and two passages from science.

The one literature passage will be on classic or contemporary literature from the U.S. or from around the world.

The passage from history and social studies will draw upon anthropology, economics, sociology and psychology, geography, law or linguistics.

The passage from founding documents or great global conversations will include content from documents important regarding the historical perspective of the US or the world.

The two passages on science will be on natural sciences such as biology, geology, archaeology, chemistry, or physics.

The paired passage will consist of two small passages, mostly by different authors but on a similar topic, linked by a common theme, on any one of the above topics.

The nature of the questions

There are broadly four categories of questions asked in SAT-Reading. However, a few question types may have two to three sub-divisions within them. We will discuss these in the next chapter.

First: **General** questions–these questions may ask you to suggest a title for the passage, or state the central idea, or identify the author's primary purpose in writing a part of a sentence or a paragraph. Another variant may be to understand the tone and style of writing used by the author.

Second: **Detail** questions–these questions ask you to understand a specific detail from the passage, or cite a fact used in the passage.

Third: **Inference** questions– these questions ask you to understand the implied meaning of the information presented by the author, or identify the intended meaning of a word or a phrase used figuratively in the passage.

Fourth: **Graphic** questions– You will see at least one graphic in the test. The graphic can contain information in the form of a table graph, chart, or some other visual clue. Questions on these graphics will require you to interpret numbers and process visual data instead of verbal. The question can either relate to the passage or be independent of it.

3.1   Reading Test Scoring

This test will get an individual test score between the range of 10-40. This Test will also contribute towards the Evidence-based Reading and Writing score with a range of 200-800, along with the Writing Test. Select questions from this test will be used to make two cross-test scores, one: Analysis in History/Social Studies, and two: Analysis in Science, both in the range of 10-40. Two of the sub-scores on the SAT, 1-15, are also based on this section: Command of Evidence and Relevant Words in Context.

3.2 Reading Strategies

(1) Fall in love with the content of the passage

Whether you love or hate the topic of the passage, you cannot ignore it. The best approach to eating that bitter fruit is to sugar-coat it with your emotions by pretending that you actually enjoy the subject and find it very interesting. In fact, frequently you will find that the SAT passages do add a lot of value to your knowledge bank.

If your mind-set is "Why should I be bothered to read about the respiratory system of sea-snakes?", keep in mind that later in your career you may be asked by your boss to summarize a report on, say, the anatomy of terrestrial animals in order for you to understand the environmental impact of some business project. So, in fact, you are actually preparing yourself for future possibilities very well by working through the reading passage in question. Alternatively, you may wish to pursue further education for which you will need to master either the GRE or GMAT, both of which will quiz you on similar passages.

Read the first paragraph very cautiously. It sets the purpose and the topic of the passage. Once you understand the topic of the passage, you should gain momentum. There are two extreme approaches to reading the passage; one: read slowly and understand each word, and two: read very fast without comprehending the meaning of the passages. Both approaches have their demerits.

The slow approach will put a lot of pressure on you, as you are likely to either blindly guess on a couple of questions due to time constraints, or panic and start committing mistakes.

The fast approach will not help you either as, for each question, you will have to reread the passage and identify the location of relevant details. With this approach, you will likely end up reading the passage at least two times without a guarantee that the questions attempted are correct. A few SAT Reading questions are not necessarily based on a particular paragraph or piece of information; they may require you to pool information from two places in the passage. Even the main point question, which is usually perceived as the one that can be answered with the reading of the first and the last paragraph, can go wrong. SAT test makers design the options in such a way that if you miss even one detail, you will get caught in their trap. So, the optimum approach is to read efficiently and effectively.

If you get a convoluted sentence, you should at least look for the main nouns and verbs, just to get a sense of the actions going on [Ask yourself: who's doing what, or who's saying what about what?]. This will gives you a broad understanding without too much detail.

At the end of the book, you will find a list of commonly used words with their meanings to improve your understanding in the Reading section.

An effective reader will read efficiently while paying attention to the message; he/she will side-line intricate details for the time being. The reader will keep in mind that some specific detail is parked in this paragraph, and, if needed, he/she will look it up there. He/she is basically a big picture reader who reads actively. The key is not to overanalyze the passage as you read it, but to get a general idea of the flow and main point of every paragraph, mentally making a map as you go along.

If you are not a native speaker of English or are not fond of reading, you may improve your reading comprehension by reading the New York Times, the Wall Street Journal, American Scientist, Popular Science, The Economist, and other competent magazines that contain SAT-like content. Another option is to frequent sites that contain research journals to enable you to read complex, data-based, verbose passages. You may also read certain novels to improve reading speed.

(2) **Keep summarizing**

The SAT passages are deliberately drafted with the use of clever language, and made convoluted to make the gist hard to grasp; often-times the data is hidden in the passage. Due to the sentence structure and style of writing, you will have to take some sort of notes to understand the nuances of the message because simply keeping the message in mind will not help.

Note-taking style is very subjective and each person has his/her own style of writing. The brief notes taken while going through test reading passages are meant only for you and only for the next 10-12 minutes of your life.

There are two distinct advantages of note-making. One, it helps you paraphrase the main point because the central message of the passage comprises all the paragraphs of the passage, and not only the first or only the first and the last. Two, you know exactly where to look for the details when needed. There may be circumstances when a specific detail for a particular question lies in two paragraphs, but your notes will guide you to look at those particular paragraphs to seek the information you need to complete the question.

You can summarize at appropriate intervals. If you are comfortable with the content, you can summarize after each paragraph; however, if you find that the content is heavy, you may opt instead to summarize after every few sentences.

Now we present to you a seemingly distasteful passage from medical science. Read the passage first, and then follow the techniques suggested by us. You will find that there is marked difference in understanding the content.

The following passage will teach you three things; one, how to read through creating impressions; two, how to retain the information from the passage; and three, how to take notes.

Passage-Cancer of the colon

Doctors are working on a new non-invasive technique that allows them to 'fly' through the colon and pick out malignancies. Admittedly the first results have been good enough for the team behind the technique to predict that it will become a universal screening system for one of the world's biggest killers. (See graph below) Thus doctors say it will detect more
5 *cancers and polyps than do conventional techniques.*

One of the predicaments with cancer of the colon is that it is difficult to detect it with great certainty with many of the current tests. If it can be detected at an early stage, treatment is much more effective. The options currently available to doctors include faecal blood testing, barium enema, and colonoscopy. Unfortunately none of these is optimal in terms
10 *of performance, safety, or patient acceptance. So Dr David Ahlquist, an oncologist at the Mayo Clinic in Minnesota, has been working on virtual-reality technology.*

Blood testing is the most widely used test at present, but it is probably the most imprecise. More than half of cancers are likely to be missed in a single test. So far based on the results of research on 70 patients, doctors have found that, despite initial programming glitches,
15 *the virtual-reality technology is far more accurate.*

Passage-inclusive graph

Here is a graph that shows the statistics on one of the world's biggest killers – cancer of the colon – and the numbers that make it one of the world's biggest killers.

The graph below represents the rates of incidence and mortality of cancer of the colon among various ethnic groups and genders in the USA.

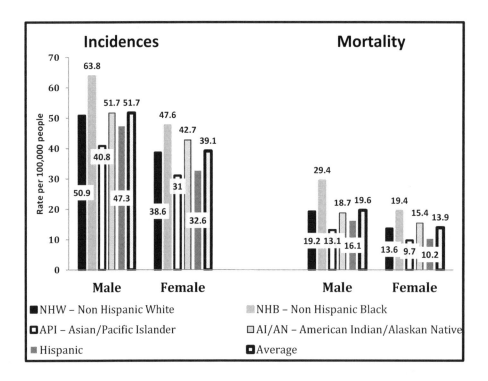

3.2.1 Reading through creating impressions

Sentence	Impression	Inference/Meaning
Doctors are working on a new non-invasive technique that allows them to 'fly' through the colon and pick out malignancies.		So far I understand that doctors are working on a new technique that does not involve incision. [because of the use of the word "non-invasive"] The rest I could not get—*fly*, and *colon*. **Gist**: Docs wkg. on non-invasive tech. on any disease (malignancies).
Admittedly the first results have been good enough for the team behind the technique to predict that		**Gist**: Non-invasive tech. ⇒ Decent success in predicting something.
it will become a universal screening system for one of the world's biggest killers.		I am sure that 'universal screening system' is used for non-invasive technique. [because of the use of "it" used for the "non-invasive technique"] It means that this technique will overcome the biggest disease (killers). **Gist**: Non-invasive tech. may detect the dreaded disease, and be accepted by all. Also, a graph containing statistics on it being one of the biggest killers is given.

Thus doctors say it will detect more cancers and polyps than do conventional techniques.		Now I know what disease is being talked about-it's CAN-CER. Well, I do not know what polyps are. I guess it must be related to cancer. The statement seems to be the main point; I must keep this in mind. **Gist**: 1. # of cancer cases > conv. tech. 2. Non-invasive tech. seems better than conv. tech..

Gist of paragraph 1: It says that doctors are working on a non-invasive technique to detect cancer of colon. It is better than the conventional technique and mostly accepted.

Paragraph 1 notes: P1: Docs wkg. on non-inv. tech.; success'l in predict'g; may detect disease; accepted; # of cancer > conv. tech.; Better.

One of the **predicaments** with cancer of the colon is that it is difficult to detect it with great certainty with many of the current tests.	Cancer of Colon 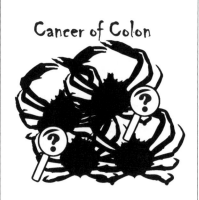	Oh, now I get that 'colon' is a body part that can get cancer! The statement states the limitation of conventional techniques. I am becoming more sure now that the previous statement must be the MAIN POINT. I must be ready for a specific question on 'cancer of the colon'. **Gist**: Current tests: Detection of cancer of the colon ⇒ difficult
If it can be detected at an early stage, treatment is much more effective.	*Early detection ⇒ Effective*	Gist: Hmm...Early detection is the key to treating 'cancer of the colon'.

The options currently available to doctors include faecal blood testing, barium enema, and colonoscopy.	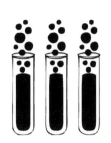	Gist: They are talking about 3 tests. I don't know what these mean.
Unfortunately none of these is optimal in terms of performance, safety, or patient acceptance.		**Gist**: 3 tests ⇒ Not reliable
So Dr David Ahlquist, an oncologist at the Mayo Clinic in Minnesota, has been working on virtual-reality technology.		Okay, so a doctor is working on virtual-reality technology. It must be one of the non-invasive techniques. Gist: A doc wkg. on virtual-reality tech. = non-invasive tech.

Gist of paragraph 2: It says that detection of colon cancer is difficult through current unreliable tests. One of the doctors is working on a virtual-reality technique, a kind of non-invasive technique.

Paragraph 2 notes: P2: Current tests: Detection of colon cancer ⇒ diff.; Early detection == key; 3 tests ⇒ unreliable; A doc wkg. on virtual-reality tech. = non-inv. tech..

Blood testing is the most widely used at present, **but** it is probably the most imprecise.		I think this fact is already stated in the II paragraph. I think the purpose may be to emphasize. **Gist**: Blood test ⇒ Not reliable

More than half of cancers are likely to be missed in a single test.	*(50%+) ⇒ Undetected*	Yes. I was right. They again emphasized the failing of the blood test technique. **Gist**: Blood test ⇒ Not reliable & deceiver
So far based on the results of research on 70 patients, doctors have found that **despite** initial programming glitches, the virtual-reality technology is far more accurate.	Paragraph 1 summary **Main Point** Paragraph 2 summary Paragraph 3 summary	Okay. So there are two points; one, virtual-reality technology is far more accurate than (conventional technique), and two, virtual-reality technology did face some programming challenges. **Gist**: Virtual-reality tech. (non-invasive tech.) is BETTER than conv. tech.. It had a few programming challenges.

Gist of paragraph 3: It says that blood test may give wrong results, and is unreliable. Virtual-reality technique gives better results than the conventional technique does.

Paragraph 3 notes: P3: Bld test ⇒ deceiver; VR tech. » conv. tech.; had challenges.

Paragraph summary

P1: Docs wkg. on non-inv. tech.; success'l in predict'g; may detect disease; accepted; # of cancer > conv. tech.; better.

P2: Current tests: Detection of colon cancer ⇒ diff.; Early detection = key; 3 tests ⇒ unreliable; A doc wkg. on virtual-reality tech. = non-inv. tech..

P3: Bld test ⇒ Deceiver; VR tech. » conv. tech.; had challenges.

(3) **Keep tabs on transition keywords**

Often the sentences used in the passages are long-winded and use modifiers, so it becomes difficult to grasp the meaning of the sentences. However, with the use of transition words, you can keep tabs on the flow and the direction of the message communicated in the passage.

Transition words such as *however, moreover, furthermore, but, therefore*, and many others tell a lot about the next sentence in relation to the previous sentence. See the following illustration to learn more about them.

Role of furthermore/moreover

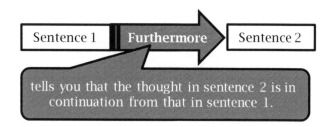

Role of however/but

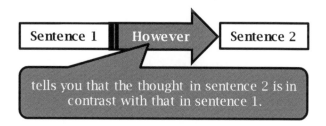

Role of therefore/hence

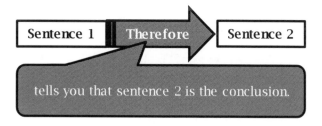

Role of If then

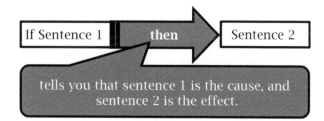

The following table of signaling or trigger words may help you understand the tone, style, and the meaning of the passage.

Continuation of thoughts	Opposing thought	Conclusion
Moreover	However	Therefore
Furthermore	But	Hence
In addition	Despite	So
Secondly	In spite of	This implies
Similarly	On the contrary	As a result
Also	Nevertheless	Thus
Too	Conversely	In short
For example	Instead	Consequently
Since	Yet	In other words
Because	Rather than	
Evidently	Still	
For instance	Surprisingly	
Illustrated by	While	
And	Although	
Analogous	Though	
Considering similar experiences	On the other hand	
	Even if	
	Actually	
	Notwithstanding	

Let us relook at the passage we read before, and identify the role of the transition words.

Doctors are working on a new non-invasive technique that allows them to 'fly' through the colon and pick out malignancies. **Admittedly** the behind the tech screening syste

> **Admittedly** shows that the next sentence is in continuation of thought from the previous sentence.

Thus conventi

> **Thus** shows that it is a conclusion from the doctors.

One of the predicaments with cancer of the colon is that it is difficult to detect it with great certainty with many of the current tests. **If** it can be detected at an early stage, treatment is much more effecti testing

> **If** shows the cause and effect relationship between the detection and the effectiveness of the treatment.

Unfortunately none of these is optimal in terms of performance, safety or patient acceptance. **So** Dr David Ahlquist, an oncologist at the Mayo nnology.

> **Unfortunately** shows the opposing thought.

> **So** shows subsequent action as a result of previous thought.

Blood testing is the it is probably the most imprecise. Mor be missed in a single test. **So far** patients, doctors has found that **despite** initial programming glitches, the virtual-reality technology ore accurate.

> **So far** shows the situation and circumstances up to now.

> **despite** shows the opposing thought.

(4) Skim the details and cut the crap

The passage may contain some technical terms which you may not know; however there is no need to know their exact meaning, but the purpose they serve in the passage is important. You should be able to tell what is being said about those technical terms. You should skim the details and cut the crap.

Let us refer to the second paragraph of the passage.

The options currently available to doctors include faecal blood testing, barium enema, and colonoscopy. Unfortunately none of these is optimal in terms of performance, safety, or patient acceptance. So Dr David Ahlquist, an oncologist at the Mayo Clinic in Minnesota, has been working on virtual-reality technology.

We find that there is no need to go into the details of currently available tests–*faecal blood testing, barium enema, and colonoscopy*. At the reading stage it is sufficient to know that there are three tests, what role they play, what the opinion is about the tests, and where in the passage these tests were quoted. You must have observed that in the paragraph summary and during the exercise of understanding the passage, we did not care much about the meaning of the technical word 'fly' and 'polyps'. The SAT test makers write the passages knowing that you may not know everything, and, moreover, there is no need to know it. The message is: skim the details.

Similarly, it is not important to know what the name of the doctor researching virtual-reality technology is, or what the name of his clinic is. You can refer to the doctor as Doc. The message is: cut the crap. If need arises to get the detail for a question, you can always go back to the specified location to do so.

(5) Abbreviate technical and difficult terms

You may come across many technical and difficult terms in the passages that may give you a headache. However, there is a way not to really see them again. Since you cannot avoid them completely, it is better to make them look more simplistic. For example, if you have trouble pronouncing the name of the doctor, abbreviate it to Dr AH. There may be a passage in which there is reference to two or more doctors, so it makes it important to know which is which, but by abbreviating, you can retain the information without getting bogged down by heavy words.

You must have observed that we grouped the three medical tests–faecal blood testing, barium enema, and colonoscopy – as '3 tests'. If we need to refer to them, we can still make them look less imposing by abbreviating them as 3 tests–FB, BE, and colon test.

(6) Infer the meaning of unfamiliar words

A passage may contain certain words which you do not know. We advise you to a develop decent vocabulary, and it can only be done through diversified reading of SAT-like content. However, you can also start with non-SAT-like content and then switch to SAT-like content.

That said, you may still be caught off guard by unfamiliar words. The good news is that every test taker comes across such words, and you can infer their meaning through the context in which they are used.

Let us see the first two paragraphs of the passage again.

Doctors are working on a new non-invasive technique that allows them to 'fly' through the colon and pick out **malignancies**. Admittedly the first results have been good enough for the team behind the technique to predict that it will become a universal screening system for one of the world's biggest killers. Thus doctors say it will detect more cancers and polyps than do conventional techniques.

*One of the **predicaments** with cancer of the colon is that it is difficult to detect it with great certainty with many of the current tests. If it can be detected at an early stage, treatment is much more effective. The options currently available to doctors include faecal blood testing, barium enema, and colonoscopy. Unfortunately none of these is optimal in terms of performance, safety, or patient acceptance. So Dr David Ahlquist, an **oncologist** at the Mayo Clinic in Minnesota, has been working on virtual-reality technology.*

Let us infer the meaning of these three words from the context of the passage.

Malignancies: Well it is difficult to infer the meaning of unknown words if they are used in the first sentence of the passage because we do not have any reference to draw from. With regards to the word—**malignancies**, the supporting phrase-'fly' through the colon and pick out **malignancies**—cannot help as 'fly' and 'colon' themselves are unfamiliar and seem to be technical terms. All we can so far infer is that doctors are able to catch **malignancies** with the use of a non-invasive technique, so **malignancies** must be something of a negative aspect for doctors to fly through and catch them with effort.

Let us see the next sentence– *Admittedly the first results have been good enough for the team behind the technique to predict **that** it will become a universal screening system for one of the world's biggest killers.*

That in bold refers to **malignancies**, while it refers to the non-invasive technique. Our inference is going in the right direction; **malignancies** must be something of a negative aspect. It may even refer to **world's biggest killers**. The next sentence helps to narrow down the meaning so we can assume that **malignancies** relates to **cancer (disease)**.

The dictionary meaning of **malignancies** is **menaces, enmities, a cancerous growth-tumour**. So, we were bang on inferring the meaning of this unknown word from the context.

Let us examine another word–**predicaments**

It is used in the sentence–*One of the **predicaments** with cancer of the colon is that it is difficult to detect it with great certainty with many of the current tests. It can be inferred that **predicaments** may be an aspect or a challenge with respect to cancer of the colon because the clause– it is difficult to detect it with great certainty–hints that it is something of a negative aspect.*

The dictionary meaning of **predicaments** is **difficulties**. Again, we were bang on inferring the meaning.

Let us see another word– **oncologist**.

It is used in the sentence– So Dr David Ahlquist, an **oncologist** at the Mayo Clinic in Minnesota, has been working on virtual-reality technology.

I think it is quite easy for you to infer the contextual meaning of **oncologist**. Even if you infer it as a **specialist**, it is fine. **Oncologist** means **cancer specialist**.

3.2.2   Active Reading

In the above passage, we saw how we can read a passage and extract its gist by "**creating impressions**" in our mind as we read. Now, let us focus a bit on more on reading aptly. The SAT test makers may offer you a scary, dense, and boring passage. They will load the passage will technical and almost indecipherable data. However, they can ask questions only on verbal data, because this is the verbal section! Hence, we must learn to read smartly to gather the right data and impressions as we read the passage. While reading the passage sentence by sentence, don't be in a hurry to understand every word. Learn to pick out the main words in a sentence (usually the nouns and the verbs). Skip around technical words and read only their initials so that your flow of thought is maintained. Pay extra attention to words of contrast and comparison, because that's where data is hidden. For most of the sentences, you will end up actually reading only fifty percent of the words, but you will fully understand the intent of the author. From a cluster of words in a sentence, pick out the main words (enough to form a sensible statement) and read only that. Initially, you may find that picking the words takes time. That is okay. Take your time to pick the words, then read the sentence made of your picked words. Repeat with the next sentence. Note making is recommended. Slowly, you will learn to pick words faster and "fly" through the passage while understanding everything.

Go over the passage again. Try to pick words and make a statement, and then compare that statement with ours in the "what I actually read" column.

We will discuss all question types in SAT-Reading in the next chapter.

Chapter 4

Question Types

 We discussed in the introduction that there are broadly four categories of questions asked in SAT-Reading. We will discuss these in detail now.

4.1 Reading Question Types

4.1.1 General

These question types can be further divided into three sub-question types. These questions can be answered after reading the passage and referring to your notes. So, in a way they save your time. You will certainly face one general question per passage on the SAT. There may be 4-5 questions based on this question type out of all the Reading questions.

4.1.1.1 Main Point

Main Point questions ask you to suggest a title for the passage, or state the main purpose of the passage. Some test prep companies also call it the **Purpose** question type.

4.1.1.2 Function

Function questions identify the role or the function of a word, phrase, sentence, or of the paragraph. It can also be called the main point of the paragraph. This type of question asks about the logical structure of a passage. Some test prep companies also call it the **Organization** or **Why** question type.

4.1.1.3 Tone

Tone questions ask you to understand the tone and style of writing used by the author.

4.1.2 Detail

These questions ask you to locate a specific detail from the passage, or cite a fact used in the passage. You have to look for the information or data with the help of keywords in the questions. These questions usually demand that you go back to the relevant portion of the passage and retrieve the data or information to answer the question. Some test prep companies also call it the**Specific** question type. There may be 3-4 questions based on this question type out of all the Reading questions.

4.1.3   Inference

These questions ask you to understand the implied meaning of the information presented by the author, or identify the intended meaning of a word or a phrase used figuratively in the passage. There may be 2-3 questions based on this question types out of all the Reading questions.

4.1.3.1   Specific Inference

This type of question asks about details from the passage. The correct answer is often a paraphrase of something directly stated in the passage. It can also ask about the use of a particular word or phrase.

4.1.3.2   Application

This is a slightly more specific type of inference question where you're asked to choose an answer which mimics a process or exemplifies a situation described in the passage. It can also be called a **Parallel reasoning** question type.

4.1.4   Reasoning

These questions are similar to assumption, and strengthen or weaken question types. You may be asked to pinpoint an underlying assumption, or strengthen or weaken a claim made by the author in the passage. There will be at least one question of this type in the Reading section.

4.1.5   Graphic

At least one graphic will be presented to you in the Reading test. Graphics can be data, quantitative or verbal, presented in visual forms. The graphics may or may not be attached to any specific passage. Questions on the graph can ask you to relate the graph information to the passage or can be based independently on the graph. The graph can also contain mathematical questions, but not of a very tough level.

4.2   Strategies to solve questions

 We know that there are four individual passages and one paired passage on the SAT Reading test. You must understand the time allocation for each passage while attempting the questions.

4.2.1   Time allocation

You know that the SAT Reading Test has 52 questions over 5 passages that you have to answer in 65 minutes. Thus, you have, in all, 13 minutes per passage, including the time taken to read the passage. Ideally, you should take 2-3 minutes to read the passage and takes notes, and, on average, 45-50 seconds to answer each question.

As soon as the test begins, go through the passages and find the one that you like or are interested in. Attempting favored passages first will ensure that you do not miss out on questions that you will find easier. Do not try to solve more than one passage at a time. Finish a passage before moving on to the next one.

> **Strategy 1:**
> *Preview all the questions; read the first question, but do not read the options.*

As stated earlier, it is a good idea to find out whether there is a question from the general question category (main point or tone question) among the questions. If there is one, you must read the passages with a purpose. Even if the passage did not ask a main point question, extracting the main point and understanding the tone of the passage will help you understand the scope of the passage better.

The approach to finding the main point is discussed in detail in the subsequent section.

4.2.2   Strategies to solve the general question

4.2.2.1   Main point question

 SAT-Reading passages are complete in themselves in communicating a thought; the content in the paragraph supports and develops a main idea or central point.

Let us see the characteristics of the main point.

(1) It is a one line statement that expresses the intent of the entire passage.

(2) It is broad in scope; it covers the entire passage and is not restricted to an example or paragraph in the passage.

(3) It is precise in scope; it usually does not contain any particular detail discussed in the passage.

Typical question stems of a main point question can be as follows:

- The primary purpose of the passage is...

- The main idea of the passage is...

- Which of the following best describes the organization of the passage?

- The passage as a whole can best be characterized as which of the following?

We will discuss how to derive the main point of a Reading passage with the help of paragraph summaries.

We have already seen the idea of a paragraph summary in a couple of examples in the previous chapter. It is a one line statement that summarizes the paragraph. The main point of a passage is a summary of paragraph summaries. It represents all the paragraphs.

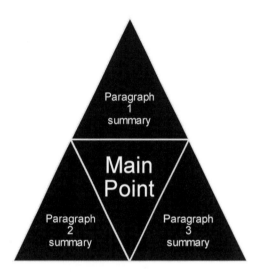

Let us see this in action. Take a look at summaries of three paragraphs of the passage **Cancer of the colon**, which we discussed in the first chapter.

Paragraph summary

P1: Docs wkg. on non-inv. tech.; success'l in predict'g; may detect disease; accepted; # of cancer > conv. tech.; better.

P2: Current tests: Detection of colon cancer ⇒ diff.; Early detection = key; 3 tests ⇒ unreliable; A doc wkg. on virtual-reality tech. = non-inv. tech..

P3: Bld test ⇒ deceiver; VR tech. » conv. tech.; had challenges.

Gist of paragraph 1: It says that doctors are working on a non-invasive technique to detect cancer of the colon. It is better than conventional techniques and mostly accepted.

Gist of paragraph 2: It says that detection of colon cancer is difficult through current un-reliable tests. One doctors is working on a virtual-reality technique, a kind of non-invasive technique.

Gist of paragraph 3: It says that blood tests may give wrong results, and are unreliable. Virtual-reality technique gives better results than the conventional technique.

The first paragraph introduces a new technique to detect colon cancer, and this technique is better than conventional ones. The second paragraph discusses that detecting colon cancer is difficult currently but the new technique, non-invasive, might turn out better. So, the second paragraph continues the first paragraph by detailing the differences between the better, new technique and unreliable, conventional techniques.

The third paragraph finishes this thought by providing specific details about how the most commonly used conventional method fails. It is hoped that the new technique (now called virtual-reality technique) will do better.

Main point: New hopes with non-invasive technique that is being researched, and disillusionment with conventional techniques for detection of cancer of colon.

> **Strategy 2:**
> *Write the main point of the passage immediately after finishing the reading of the passage.*

> **Strategy 3:**
> *Make sure that main points of each paragraph are represented in the main point of the passage.*

> **Strategy 4:**
> *Be wary of extreme words like most, all, always, never, etc., in the options.*

Let us see a main point question with some options from the **Cancer of the Colon** passage. You can refer to the passage in the first chapter—Introduction.

Question 1 — General, main point

The author is primarily concerned with

(A) The difficulties involved in detecting cancer — the biggest killer.

(B) Virtual reality cancer testing techniques for colon cancer.

(C) Existing technique problems and new technique possibilities.

(D) Colon cancer detection techniques and problems.

Solution

Based on the above deductions, we can analyze the options one by one.

(A)   This option is **incorrect** because this option is too general. The passage is not discussing "cancer" in general. The scope of the passage is only "colon cancer".

(B)   This option is **incorrect** because while the passage is discussing the new, non-invasive technique (virtual reality technique), it's not discussing only that. The passage also mentions the lack of success of conventional techniques.

(C)   This option is **correct** because it clearly outlines all the main issues discussed in the passage - the lack of success of conventional techniques and hope of success with the new, non-invasive technique.

(D)   This option is **incorrect** because while this option is close, it's too general. The passage does discuss colon cancer detection techniques. However, the passage distinguishes between conventional and new, innovative techniques, but this option does not convey that. Also, this option implies that all techniques for colon cancer detection have problems, but the passage conveys that conventional techniques are problematic, but the new one is possibly going to solve the problems.

The correct answer is C.

4.2.2.2   Function questions

 Organization, or function, questions ask you why the author wrote a particular paragraph, sentence, or even word. The answer to these questions depends on the context of the passage or the issue at hand. The answer to the question will lie around the word or in the sentence; you will have to look at the previous sentence or the succeeding sentence to get the information. In 'Why' questions you have to think broadly and ask what role the word or the sentence used in the context plays.

Typical question stems of a function question are as follows.

· The author mentions < something > in the third paragraph in order to...

· One of the functions of the second paragraph is to...

· The highlighted word in the first paragraph is used by the author in order to...

· The discussion of < something > is meant to...

Let us look at some examples.

Examine another question from the Cancer of the colon passage. You can refer to the passage in the first chapter—Introduction.

Question 2 — General, function

What purpose does the second paragraph serve with respect to the passage on the whole?

(A) It explains why the new technique will be more successful than the conventional one

(B) It provides the main point of the passage

(C) It presents one of the main reasons for development of the innovative technique

(D) It provides explanations for why conventional techniques are problematic

Solution

The above question asks us to find the purpose of the second paragraph with respect to the whole passage. This is a function question from the general category. We have to figure out what function the second paragraph serves in the bigger scheme of things.

The first paragraph introduces the new technique under development.

The second paragraph contains information about conventional techniques. However, at the end of second paragraph lies the reason behind mentioning the given information — "Unfortunately none of these is optimal in terms of performance, safety, or patient acceptance. So Dr David Ahlquist, an oncologist at the Mayo Clinic in Minnesota, has been working on virtual-reality technology." Thus the given information is serving the purpose of explaining why Dr David has been working on a virtual-reality technique.

The third and final paragraph explains why hopes are pinned on this new technique.

The purpose of the passage is to present the hopes for the new technique and the disillusionment with conventional techniques.

Thus the second paragraph provides an excellent basis for the development of the new technique.

Let's analyze the options one by one.

(A) This option is **incorrect** because the second paragraph does not state that the new technique will be more successful, but the third paragraph does.

(B) This option is **incorrect** because discussing only the conventional techniques is not the main point of the passage. The main point is "colon cancer detection techniques and problems". The second paragraph discusses only the conventional techniques in general.

(C) This option is **correct** because the last line (So far....accurate) of the second paragraph does provide this clue. The details of the conventional technique are given to explain why the need for a new technique exists. This is the paragraph's purpose in the passage — to explain why the new technique in under development.

(D) This option is **incorrect** because while the paragraph provides information about conventional techniques and their problematic nature, that is not the purpose of the paragraph. It does not provide explanations. The purpose of the paragraph is to explain why Dr. David is developing the virtual-reality technique. [This is substantiated by the "so" sentence]. This option is tricky because it contains an answer for "what is presented in the second paragraph?" but this option does not answer "why is the second paragraph present in the passage?"

The correct answer is C.

4.2.2.3 Tone questions

 The tone of a passage is the author's emotion or feeling, associated with his content. The style is the particular way the author uses language to articulate the content. Most style or tone questions will include the words 'attitude,' 'tone,' 'style,' 'feeling,' etc. The most important thing you should do while reading a Reading Comprehension passage is to understand the author's tone. Some information in the passage will come from the author's attitude and writing style.

The way modulation plays an important role in speech, tone plays a role in understanding the intent of the words written by the author. Adjectives and adverbs used by the author to express his emotions form the tone and style because they are openly expressive.

Tones can be categorized into three broad types:

Explanatory, Analytical, and Opinionated.

Explanatory: This can also be considered the **Descriptive** tone. The author does not offer any opinion, recommendation, or analysis of the issue at hand.

Analytical: This is the tone when the author wants to analyze a situation, topic, or problem. The tone will not necessarily be explicit, but it will contain some subjective paragraphs, sentences, or phrases with the usage of suggestive adjectives and adverbs.

Opinionated: The tone can be characterized as opinionated if the author clearly expresses his feelings and emotions while presenting his views or evaluating a theory.

Let us see a paragraph written with a **neutral** tone.

The Morton and Jackson Company registered a 2.58% growth rate in the third and the fourth quarters. During the same period, the industry clocked a 10.28% growth rate. The management and the CEO are figuring out what caused the growth rate.

You may have observed that the paragraph is written to convey information about the performance of the Morton and Jackson Company in the third and the fourth quarters. It doesn't explain or analyze the cause, and it doesn't offer any opinion.

Let us see the same paragraph written with an **opinionated** tone.

It is ironic that the Morton and Jackson Company registered a dismal growth rate in the third and the fourth quarters despite the industry having reached an unduly high double-digit growth rate. It is a matter of grave concern that, in spite of its much acclaimed performance in the first and the second quarters, the company is going downhill.

The passage is presented to you again with suggestive adjectives and adverbs highlighted. These will help you sense the emotions and feeling associated with them.

*It is **ironic** that the Morton and Jackson Company registered a **dismal** growth rate in the third and the fourth quarters despite the industry having reached an unduly high double-digit growth rate. It is a matter of **grave concern** that, in spite of a much **acclaimed** performance in the first and the second quarters, the company is going **downhill**.*

Let us see the same paragraph written with an **analytical** tone.

The Morton and Jackson Company registered a 2.58% growth rate in the third and the fourth quarters; however, the industry clocked a 10.28% growth rate during the same period. There are contradicting theories flying around in the company to understand the dip of 7.7% points in the growth rate; on one hand, the management blames inefficient operations, alluding that the onus lies on the CEO; on the other hand, the CEO accuses the workers' union of a 'Go-Slow' method of striking. It cannot be decided without acquiring some information about both sides of the story.

The passage is presented to you again with suggestive adjectives, adverbs, and phrases highlighted. These will help you sense the implied intent of the author.

*The Morton and Jackson Company registered a 2.58% growth rate in the third and the fourth quarters; however, the industry clocked a 10.28%growth rate during the same period. There are contradicting theories flying around in the company to **understand the dip of 7.7% points in the growth rate**; on one hand, the management blames **inefficient operations, alluding that the onus lies on the CEO**; on the other hand, the **CEO accuses the workers' union of a 'Go-Slow' method of striking**. It cannot be decided without acquiring some information about both sides of the story.*

Let us see the same paragraph written with an **explanatory** tone.

The Morton and Jackson Company's 2.58% growth rate in the third and the fourth quarters despite the industry's 10.28% growth rate during the same period is understandable. The management's wish to make the CEO accountable for the low growth rate is natural because the responsibility of efficient operations lies with the CEO. The CEO wishes to make the workers' union accountable for the low growth rate since the responsibility of efficient operations lies with the union.

The passage is presented to you again with the relevant sentences highlighted. Reading the passage, you will sense that the author's intent is to explain the causes.

*The Morton and Jackson Company's 2.58% growth rate in the third and the fourth quarters despite the industry's 10.28% growth rate during the same period is understandable. The management's wish to make the CEO accountable for the low growth rate is natural **because** the responsibility of efficient operations lies with the CEO. The CEO wishes to make the workers' union accountable for the low growth rate **since** the responsibility of efficient operations lies with the union.*

At the end of the book, you will find a comprehensive glossary of tones used in the Reading Comprehension passage.

Typical question stems of a Tone question are as follows.

* The tone of the passage can be best described as...

> **Strategy 5:**
> *Write one or two words in short hand describing the tone of the passage immediately after finishing reading it.*

> **Strategy 6:**
> *Don't be swayed by a couple of suggestive adjectives or adverbs; judge the tone from the context as a whole.*

Let us look at an example with another question from the **Cancer of the colon** passage. You can refer to the passage given in the first chapter—Introduction.

Question 3 — Tone

According to the passage, the tone of the author towards the conventional techniques mentioned in the passage can be best described as

(A) Qualified approval

(B) Ruthless criticism

(C) Half-hearted acceptance

(D) Disillusionment and lack of trust

Solution

The question asks us to ascertain the tone of the author towards the conventional techniques. This is a tone question from the general category.

The author is clearly not analytical or explanatory, but is opinionated, as evidenced by use of words like "unfortunately", "admittedly", etc. The author is not neutral or positive towards the conventional techniques. He uses a negative tone regarding the conventional methods with the word "unfortunately" included. However, he does not criticize the techniques; he merely presents the fact that the tests are imprecise and unreliable.

Let's go over the options one by one.

(A) This option is **incorrect** because the author does not approve, but disapproves of the conventional techniques.

(B) This option is **incorrect** because the author does not ruthlessly (viciously and cruelly) criticize the techniques, but points out that they're not useful and are inaccurate.

(C) This option is **incorrect** because the author does not accept the techniques, but rather disapproves of them.

(D) This option is **correct** because the author does express disillusionment with the lack of success of the conventional techniques and does not trust them because he calls them imprecise and unreliable.

The correct answer is D.

4.2.3 Strategies to solve Detail questions

 As the name suggests, Detail questions ask about the details in the passage. Your task is to locate a detail asked in the question in the relevant portion of the passage. It is likely that the words or the phrases used in the question do not match those in the portion of the passage; however, having understood the meaning from the question, look for the detail in the passage. Most of the time, the correct answer is a restatement of part of the passage.

Frequently test makers make options that are true according to the passage and seem attractive, but they may not be relevant to the question asked. Your task is to find the details not only true with respect to the passage, but also relevant to the question.

Sometimes the information you need is cleverly hidden by the author. It may be possible that the correct option is a rephrasing of the specific detail, but is written in such a convoluted manner that you do not realize that it is what you want.

Typical question stems of a Detail question are as follows:

 · According to the passage, the author suggests which of the following to...

 · According to the passage, the reason for <detail> is due to...

 · The author quotes all the following as a <danger to mankind> EXCEPT...

Strategy 7:
Any true detail is not necessarily the answer; the details must be true as well as relevant.

Let us look at an example with another question from the **Cancer of the colon** passage. You can refer to the passage given in the first chapter—Introduction.

Question 4 — Detail

According to the passage, the author would most likely agree with which of the following as an advantage of virtual-reality testing over conventional methods?

(A) It is completely reliable and yields precise results.

(B) It has been adopted as the standard test throughout the world.

(C) It can detect cancerous growth at an earlier stage than can conventional testing.

(D) Surgical invasion is not required to obtain results.

Solution

The question is to find some detail about virtual-reality testing that the author will agree is an advantage over conventional methods.

Let's go over the options one by one.

(A) This option is **incorrect** because while the author says that the conventional methods are unreliable, he does not necessarily say that the virtual reality technique is completely reliable. In fact, he calls the technique "far more accurate" but not "completely accurate".

(B) This option is **incorrect** because the technique is still being tested and could not have been adopted all over the world.

(C) This option is **incorrect** because we cannot infer whether it can detect cancerous growth at an earlier stage than can conventional testing. All we can say is that the new technique is more accurate.

(D) This option is **correct** because this can be inferred from the passage. The author mentions that the technique is "non-invasive".

The correct answer is D.

4.2.4   Strategies to solve Inference questions

 Inference questions ask you to draw an inference from a word, phrase, or sentence used in context. You have to understand the implied meaning unstated by the author, but it **must be true** according to the passage.

These questions pose a challenge, as the required information may be found in several places in the passage, and you have to group them together to make a must-be-true inference.

Detail questions and Inference questions are logically the same, as both ask for the must-be-true detail from the passage, but Inference questions go beyond what is written in the passage. They ask you to infer or imply what is not written, yet is true according to the passage.

The key is not to infer something that is true in real-life, but something that is necessarily true as per the passage. Be confined to the boundary of the passage.

Typical question stems of Inference question are as follows:

- · The author would most likely agree with which of the following...

- · It can be inferred from the passage that...

- · The passage suggests that < something > may cause < something > if...

Strategy 8:
Beware of real-world truth traps; stay confined to the scope of the passage.

Strategy 9:
Infer the least, and justify all the relevant information; do not satisfy yourself with 'could be true'; strive for 'must be true'.

Strategy 10:
Beware of boundary line words (extreme words); be skeptical.

Let us look at some examples with more questions from the **Cancer of the colon** passage. You can refer to the passage given in the first chapter—Introduction.

Question 5 — Specific Inference

According to the passage, which of the following can be inferred?

(A) This technique will make curing colon cancer a relatively simple task.

(B) More than half of cancers go undetected.

(C) There are only three alternatives to virtual reality screening.

(D) Detection is only one of the problems in the treatment of colon cancer.

Solution

The question is to find the correct inference. This is a specific inference question from the Inference category.

Let's go over the options one by one.

(A) This option is **incorrect** because the technique is meant only for detection and not for curing colon cancer. After detection, there may be other complications in the treatment.

(B) This option is **incorrect** because it is too extreme. We cannot say how many cancers go undetected. All we know is that colon cancer is one of the biggest killers and that detecting it early is one of the problems. However, we don't know all the problems or the other cancer types and their detection rates.

(C) This option is **incorrect** because the passage states that "currently" three alternatives are available, implying that there have been more alternatives in the past and may be more in the future.

(D) This option is **correct** because the first line of the second paragraph (One of the predicaments ... current tests) affirms this fact. The detection of colon cancer is one of the problems. Treatment can have other complications, too.

The correct answer is D.

Let us look at another example.

Question 6 — Specific Inference

Which of the following is closest in meaning and context to the word "optimal" as used in Line 9 ("Unfortunately ... acceptance") in the first paragraph?

(A) superlative

(B) adequate

(C) inefficacious

(D) dubious

Solution

We need to find the word closest to "optimal" as used in the passage. The sentence is "*Unfortunately, none of these (the three tests) is **optimal** in terms of performance, safety, and patient-acceptance.*" Thus, the tests are not "optimal" or "satisfactory" in performance or safety and are not accepted by patients. Thus, "optimal" is used to describe a satisfactory level of safety and performance.

Let's analyze the options one by one.

(A) This option is **incorrect** because "superlative" means "the best"; however, "optimal" does not need to be "the best", but only "optimal" or "satisfactory".

(B) This option is **correct** because "adequate" can be used as "satisfactory".

(C) This option is **incorrect** because "inefficacious" means "not producing the desired result" and cannot be close to "acceptable" or "optimal". It is the opposite of what is needed.

(D) This option is **incorrect** because "dubious" means "doubtful/unlikely to work", but we need a word close to "acceptable" not "unlikely to work". It is the opposite of what is needed.

The correct answer is B.

4.2.5   Strategies to solve Reasoning-based questions

 You will see at least one question from this category in every passage that you encounter. You may be asked to identify the underlying assumption of the conclusion by the author, or which piece of information can make the conclusion strong or weak.

Typical question stems of Inference question are as follows:

· Which of the following, if true, would help conclude < something >?

· Which of the following, if true, would undermine the conclusion < something >?

· Which of the following was implied while concluding < something >?

Let us look at some examples with more questions from the **Cancer of the colon** passage. You can refer to the passage given in the first chapter—Introduction.

Question 7 — Reasoning

Which of the following, if true, would most weaken the implications of the last sentence of the passage, keeping it in perspective of the passage?

(A)   Programming glitches, if unresolved, can influence the results of the program.

(B)   Patients are not always enthusiastic about virtual reality programs, especially in cases of serious illnesses.

(C)   Setting up virtual-reality scanners will be quite expensive, even if it's only a one-time cost.

(D)   Blood testing can detect colon cancers usually when the cancer has been around for one and a half years.

Solution

The question is to weaken the last line of the passage. So, this is a reasoning question. The last line is "So far based on the results of research on 70 patients, doctors have found that despite initial programming glitches, the virtual-reality technology is far more accurate." The last sentence explains that the virtual reality technique is far more accurate, but some programming glitches need to be worked out. This is based on results obtained from 70 patients. Any information that weakens the conclusion that this technique is more accurate will be the answer.

Let's go over the options one by one.

(A) This option is **correct** because if this is true, then the programming glitches might have influenced the results and the accuracy of the results might not be necessarily true.

(B) This option is **incorrect** because patients' enthusiasm will not affect the technique's accuracy or results.

(C) This option is **incorrect** because cost is not mentioned as an issue at all in the passage, and, thus, this is out of scope.

(D) This option is **incorrect** because we know that blood tests are imprecise and don't yield accurate results. From what point of time they detect anything is irrelevant to the virtual reality technique.

The correct answer is A.

Question 8 — Reasoning

Which of the following provides the best evidence for the statement that the most widely used technique is the most ineffective?

(A) Line 12 ("Blood testing .... most imprecise")

(B) Lines 8-9 ("The options currently ... colonoscopy")

(C) Lines 12-13 ("More than half ... a single test")

(D) Lines 4-5 ("Thus, the doctors say ... conventional techniques")

Solution

We have been asked to find a sentence that provides evidence and adds support to the statement that the most widely used technique is the most ineffective. From the first sentence of the second paragraph (line 12), we know that blood testing is the most widely used one and is the most imprecise. This sentence is supported by the statement immediately followed by it (lines 12-13), which explains that more than half of all cancers are undetected by blood tests.

Let's analyze the options one by one.

(A) This option is **incorrect** because this sentence does not support the statement; it merely makes the same statement.

(B) This option is **incorrect** because it merely presents the three options available to doctors, but does not discuss their ineffectiveness.

(C) This option is **correct** because it provides evidence showing that blood testing, the most widely used test, is ineffective in detecting cancers.

(D) This option is **incorrect** because it simply states that the new technique is better than the old technique, but it does not add support to the statement that blood testing is the most widely used technique and is the most imprecise.

The correct answer is C.

Question 9 — Reasoning

Which of the following, if true, would most strengthen the implications of the last sentence of the second paragraph in the passage (lines 13-15), keeping it in the context of the passage?

(A) Patients do not readily yield to the results obtained by virtual-reality technology.

(B) The seventy researched patients included every variety of demographic that can be represented.

(C) The seventy patients did not include patients who suffer from other disorders that affect detection of cancers.

(D) Virtual-reality scanners will be as expensive as MRI machines to set up.

Solution

The question is to strengthen the last line of the second paragraph. So, this is a reasoning question. The sentence is "*So far based on the results of research on 70 patients, doctors have found that despite initial programming glitches, the virtual-reality technology is far more accurate.*" The last sentence states that the virtual reality technique is far more accurate, but some programming glitches need to be worked out. This is based on results obtained from 70 patients. Any information that strengthens the conclusion that this technique is more accurate will be the answer.

Let's analyze the options one by one.

(A) This option is **incorrect** because patients' responses are irrelevant to the accuracy of the tests.

(B) This option is **correct** because this can strengthen the conclusion that this technique is more accurate, since the conclusion is based on research on 70 patients. If those 70 patients accurately represent the population at large, the conclusion will hold true for the population.

(C) This option is **incorrect** because this weakens the conclusion that this technique is more accurate, since the conclusion is based on research on 70 patients. If those 70 patients do not include all types of patients in the population at large, the conclusion will not necessarily hold true for the population, especially if there are disorders that affect cancer detection and patients exhibiting such disorders were not included in the study.

(D) This option is **incorrect** because cost is not mentioned in the passage and is out of scope.

The correct answer is B.

4.2.6   Graphic Questions

At least one Reading passage in the SAT Reading test will include graphics such as a table, pictogram or graph. The information will be presented in a visual way, rather than a verbal way. Sometimes information will be quantitative, including numbers and amounts, to convey some meaning. Graph questions can be based entirely on the graphic itself or can ask you to relate the information to the relevant sentences in the passage.

Always relate the answer choices to the graph and check whether the choice holds true according to the graph and the passage. Be careful not to assume any information not given in the graph.

The graph below represents the rate of incidence and rate of mortality as per race and gender in the USA.

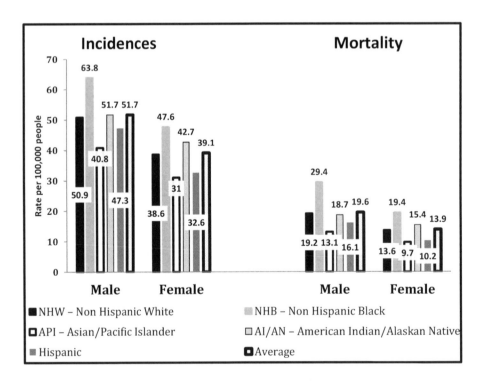

Question 10 – Graphical

According to the passage above and the graph, all of the following categories have a higher rate of incidence of cancer of the colon than that of female American Indian/Alaskan natives, EXCEPT

(A) Non-Hispanic black males

(B) Asian males

(C) Hispanic males

(D) Non-Hispanic white males

Solution

The question asks us to find that category whose rate of incidence of cancer of the colon is *less* than that of female American Indian/Alaskan natives. The rate of incidence of cancer of the colon in female American Indian/Alaskan natives is 42.7. We'll compare this rate with that of the categories given in the options.

Let's analyze the options one by one.

(A) This option is **incorrect** because the rate of incidence of cancer of the colon in Non-Hispanic black males is 63.8, which is higher than the rate of incidence of cancer of the colon in female Alaskan natives.

(B) This option is **correct** because the rate of incidence of cancer of the colon in Asian males is 40.8, which is not higher than the rate of incidence of cancer of the colon in female Alaskan natives.

(C) This option is **incorrect** because the rate of incidence of cancer of the colon in Hispanic males is 47.3, which is higher than the rate of incidence of cancer of the colon in female Alaskan natives.

(D) This option is **incorrect** because the rate of incidence of cancer of the colon in Non-Hispanic white males is 50.9, which is higher than the rate of incidence of cancer of the colon in female Alaskan natives.

The correct answer is B.

Question 11 — Graphical; Calculation-based

According to the information from the graph, which of the following statements is correct?

(A) There is only one group in which the number of incidences of cancer of the colon for females is more than that for males.

(B) There are exactly four groups in which the number of mortalities of cancer of the colon for males is more than that for females.

(C) Hispanic males are closer to non-Hispanics white males than they are to non-Hispanics black males in the likelihood of vulnerability to cancer of the colon or succumbing to it.

(D) For the number of incidences of cancer of the colon or the number of mortalities from cancer of the colon, the Hispanic group is the most similar to the average group.

Solution

Since we have to select one option as the correct answer, let us analyze each option one by one.

(A) The option means that among 5 groups – NHW, NHB, API, AI/AN, and Hispanic – there is exactly one group for which the number of incidences of cancer for females is more than that for males.

We must focus on the first two clusters of the graph as they belong to 'Incidences'.

Let us do a like to like comparison. We find that NHW male number (50.9) is more than the corresponding NHW female number (38.6); NHB male is 63.8, which is more than the corresponding NHB female at 47.6; and similarly for the remaining three groups, the figures for males are higher than those for females, so there is NO group in which the number of incidences of cancer of the colon for females is more than that for males. So this option is **incorrect**.

(B) Now we must focus on the last two clusters of the graph as they belong to 'mortality'.

As we did in option A, let us do a like to like comparison. We find that the NHW male number (19.2) is more than the corresponding NHW female number (13.6); NHB male (29.4) is more than the corresponding NHB female (19.4); and similarly for the remaining three groups, the figures for males are higher than those for females, so there are exactly five, and not four, groups in which the number of mortalities from cancer of the colon for males is more than that for females. So this option is **incorrect**.

(C) In simpler terms, the option statement means that whether one is evaluating Hispanics and the number of incidences or evaluating the number of mortalities, they are more like non-Hispanic whites than non-Hispanic blacks.

Let us look at the first two clusters (Incidences).

The number of NHW males is 50.9, the number of NHB males is 63.8, and the number of Hispanic males is 47.3. Since 47.3 is closer to 50.9 than to 63.8, we can conclude that for 'incidences' Hispanic males are more like NHW males.

Let us look at the first two clusters (Mortality).

The number of NHW males is 19.2, the number of NHB males is 29.4, and the number of Hispanic males is 16.1. Since 16.1 is closer to 19.2 than to 29.4, we can conclude that for 'mortality' too, Hispanic males are more like NHB. So option C is the **correct** answer.

(D) Though we know the correct answer is C, let's discuss option D for better understanding.

The option statement means that whether for 'incidences' or 'mortality', the figures for the Hispanic group are the closest to the corresponding figures for averages.

We see that the number of AI/AN males for 'Incidences' is 51.7, and the corresponding average is also 51.7, so for 'incidences', AI/AN males and not Hispanic males are similar, thus we need not do further analysis. This option is **incorrect**.

The correct answer is C.

Now, we should be well-versed in passage reading, question types, and their strategies.

Let us try the same on the practice questions that follow in the next chapter.

Chapter 5

SAT-like Practice Passages

5.1 Passage 1 (Climate change by volcanic eruptions)

(From a text published in 1999)

Iceland is one of the most volcanic places on the planet, with over 160 volcanoes, and it experiences a major volcanic eruption almost every decade. The close proximity to Europe and the prevailing western winds makes it possible for volcanic ash and gases to reach the continent. One of the most notable and best documented events was the eruption of the Laki Volcano in 1873. The eruption started on 8 June and lasted for eight months, producing 15 cubic kilometers of lava.

There have been many previous studies that have focused on understanding the potential role of Icelandic volcanic eruptions in modifying the environment; they have concentrated on the degree of induced climate change; however, the complex interaction of the processes which control the atmospheric circulation patterns of the earth were imperfectly understood when such studies were being conducted, and even with advanced equipment have proved difficult to model. Thus, the studies have not taken into account these complex interactions when looking at the role of Icelandic volcanic eruptions in affecting the environment and bringing about climate change.

One of the main ideas put forth is that in 1783, volcanic gases emitted by the eruption in Iceland were transported to Europe by the prevailing winds, where they caused considerable respiratory distress to susceptible people, and damage to crops, trees and fish. Documentary evidence suggests that during the Laki fissure eruption, severe acid damage to crops occurred in northern Europe and acid pulses killed fish in Scotland as the discharge of sulfuric and hydrofluoric acid continued over many weeks after the initial eruptions. These studies also propose that upper troposphere and lower stratosphere aerosols from Laki disrupted the thermal balance of the Arctic regions for two summers, and were the main mechanism for the associated climate perturbations . Although an induced climatic change that was the result of the volcanic eruption was probably the primary mechanism responsible for the main damage to crops and ecology in the surrounding area, the degree to which atmospheric circulation of winds responds to volcanic eruption and forcing is uncertain, so it is unsatisfactory to suggest that stress in the palaeo-environmental record, associated with a volcanic eruption, has inevitably occurred in response to volcanic forcing of climate. The only volcanic erup-

47

tions which possess the theoretical ability to bring about climate change are those which emit substantial volumes of volatile gases. "Climate change theories" require that these gases be injected into the stratosphere and remain in the troposphere. They must inevitably settle and be deposited on the surrounding sea and land rather than distant ecosystems. Despite plenty of
50   excavations, such sedimentary evidence still eludes researchers around the Laki central fissure.

Admittedly, many crops withered because of the acid deposition, but there are no reports on the continent of famine. This was different in northern Scotland, where the population was facing hardship because of a harvest failure in 1782, a year before the eruption. The food
55   situation was already poor when acid deposition and ash from the Laki eruption rained down and destroyed crops. Reports from northern Scotland suggest that many farmers and their families abandoned their farms and 'were forced to beg or perish'. This shows that the effects of the Laki eruption were not the direct cause of famine in Northern Scotland, but the last straw which triggered the crisis.
60
Thus, perhaps the 1873 Laki eruption contributed to more serious consequences for the Icelandic population. Iceland depended heavily on sheep and cattle herding as a source of food production, along with some production of grain and other crops. Acid deposition stunted the growth of grass, affecting fodder production to feed animals during the winter months. In ad-
65   dition, fluorine deposition poisoned streams and grass, killing around 80 percent of sheep and half of all cattle. As a result, an estimated 20-25 percent of the population died in the famine and fluorine poisoning after the fissure eruptions ceased. Volcanic eruptions are inadequate to explain social and ecological changes. Climatic and environmental disasters are, most of the time, "funnels", and not direct causes of long term historical developments. They reinforce
70   already existing historical patterns, such as migration or political instability, over exploitation or the development of new economic and social regimes.

Question 1

The author is primarily concerned with

(A) discussing various theories concerning volcanoes and climate change

(B) providing evidence that explains climate change in Europe with volcanic eruption

(C) refuting the suggestion that climate change occurred due to volcanic eruption

(D) rejecting a controversial hypothesis about the climate change phenomena in Europe

Question 2

According to the passage, which of the following can be concluded about previous studies of volcanic eruptions?

(A) The paleo-environmental record suggested positively that volcanoes were responsible.

(B) The findings were invalidated by accepted climate change theories.

(C) The findings are difficult to support with evidence and can't be conclusively determined.

(D) Volcanic eruptions are likely to have brought about induced environmental changes.

Question 3

Which of the following is best supported by the passage with regard to the volcanic eruptions in 1783?

(A) The emissions forced climate change by raising the temperature of the atmosphere.

(B) Volcanic emissions were injected into the stratosphere and then the troposphere.

(C) It modified the climate of Northern Europe.

(D) Attempts to link it with climate change have not been substantiated yet.

Question 4

According to the passage, what evidence, if provided, would suggest that Icelandic volcanic activity has been a force for environmental change and would prove the author incorrect?

(A) Volcanic emissions deposited on sea and land around Northern Europe

(B) Environmental stress induced by the paleo-environmental record

(C) Written accounts of dead fish in Scotland and crop damage in Germany

(D) Induced climatic fluctuation documented in Northern and Western Europe

Question 5

In the given passage, what is the purpose of the second paragraph with respect to the third and fourth paragraphs?

(A) To lay the groundwork for the implication that volcanic eruptions lack the environmental stress to induce climate change

(B) To explain how Laki fissure eruptions could have affected crops and fish in Northern Europe

(C) To prove that volcanic eruptions cannot bring about induced climate change because they lack the environmental pressure

(D) To explain how volcanic eruptions can bring about induced climate change in specific cases

Question 6

According to the context of the passage, the highlighted word **perturbations** is closest in meaning to which of the following options?

(A) Activity

(B) Turmoil

(C) Repression

(D) Domination

Question 7

Which of the following sentences from the final paragraph provides substantiation to the statement that the Laki volcano eruption affected the Icelandic population?

(A)   Line 45-46 ("Thus, perhaps ... Icelandic population.")

(B)   Line 46-47 ("Iceland depended ... and other crops.")

(C)   Line 48-50 ("In addition ... half of all cattle.")

(D)   Line 51-53 ("Volcanic eruptions ... historical developments.")

Question 8

Which of the following would best sum up the author's view about the connection between the Laki volcano and the situation in Northern Scotland?

(A)   It was the main cause of the terrible situation of Scotland.

(B)   It exacerbated an already bad state of affairs.

(C)   It brought about ecological changes.

(D)   It was responsible for the famine in the region.

Question 9

The author discusses the crop situation in the first line of the fourth paragraph primarily in order to

(A)   dispute the claim that the eruption caused a crisis in Europe

(B)   acknowledge the extent of the effects of the volcanic eruption

(C)   suggest that the famine can be only partly blamed on the eruption

(D)   explain how the volcano affected the population in Europe

The following two questions are based on the following bar chart.

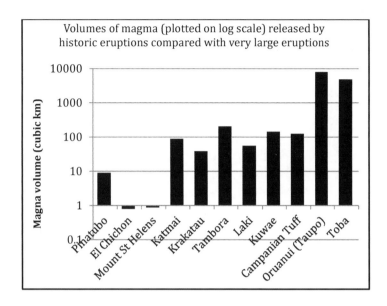

Question 10

Which of the 11 volcanic eruptions represents median magna volume (cubic km)?

(A) Laki

(B) Krakatau

(C) Kuwae

(D) Katmai

Question 11

Which of the following pairs of volcanic eruptions have the least difference between their magna volumes?

(A) Toba & Oruanui

(B) Mount St Helen & Oruanui

(C) Kuwae & Campanian Tuff

(D) Laki & Tambora

5.2   Passage 2 (In-fighting Indian princes and the rise of the British)

For 17th century Europeans, the history of Eastern monarchies, like everything else in Asia, was stereotyped and invariable. According to accounts of Indian events, history unfolded itself with the predictable rituals of heavy-handed folklore. Typically, the founder of a dynasty, a brave soldier, is a desperate intriguer, and expels from the throne the feeble and degener-
5   ate scions of a more ancient house. This founder's son may inherit some of the talent of the father, but in two or three generations, luxury and indolence do their work, and the feeble inheritors of a great name are dethroned by some new adventurer, destined to bequeath a like misfortune to his degenerate descendants. Thus rebellion and deposition were the correctives of **despotism**, and, therefore, a recurrence, at fixed intervals, of able and vigorous princes
10   through the medium of periodical anarchy and civil war, occurred. It was this perception of history that allowed Britain's rulers to lay claim to the governance of the subcontinent. The British claimed to be interested in avoiding these periods of bloodshed. This claim justified British policy, as well as dictated how they thought about gaining the favor of India's local monarchies. The rationale that justified their actions to the British public was that avoiding
15   such upheaval to allow peaceful reign over India was their ultimate goal.

British armies and British administrators were able to insinuate rule over India by two primary methods. The first of these was the outright annexation of Indian states and subsequent direct governance of the underlying regions. The second form of asserting power involved
20   treaties in which Indian rulers acknowledged the Company's hegemony in return for limited internal autonomy. Since the Company operated under financial constraints, it had to set up political underpinnings for its rule. The most important such support came from the subsidiary alliances with Indian princes during the first 75 years of Company rule. The British achieved this by setting up native princes in positions of power. Their methods took advantage
25   of existing "doctrines of lapse", and made use of what was already the declared law in cases of heredity. By intervening on behalf of one prince or another, both of whom may have been equally suited to claim the right to the throne in cases in which the rights to leadership lapsed, they put themselves in a position to support a leader they selected, and to maintain his power as long as it was in their interests. In this way the princes became practically obliged to
30   cooperate with the British. The result was two generations of petty despots, insulated from the consequences of misrule by British bayonets. The despots spent their lives in listless debauchery, broken by paroxysms of cruelty and oppression.

Question 1

It can be inferred from the passage that Britain was easily able to impose a proxy rule on the Indian subcontinent because of:

(A)   a lack of corruption within the British administration

(B)   the deployment of well-trained British soldiers

(C)   superior weaponry

(D)   the use of pre-existing laws of leadership lapses

Question 2

The author of the passage would be likely to agree with which of the following statements?

(A) British intervention in India left it no worse off than when the British arrived

(B) British intervention in India was a positive influence on India

(C) The system of rule in India before the British arrived had no faults

(D) India would have been better off to carry out its cycle of lapse and renewal without British influence

Question 3

The attitude of the author towards the reported cycle of rule in Asian and British tactics can best be described as:

(A) Disparaging

(B) Despair

(C) Skepticism

(D) Approval

Question 4

The damage caused by British rule to the subcontinent was effected by

(A) the inability of the people to choose their leader

(B) the inability of the people to resist oppression

(C) the demoralization of the Indian identity

(D) the exploitative nature of the relationship between Britain and the princes

Question 5

One judgment about the British offered by this passage might be that

(A) they were interested exclusively in exploiting India's resources

(B) they got involved in governing colonies which they knew were beyond their powers of governance

(C) they had a benign influence on India

(D) they sought practical opportunity when their self-interest matched local rulers' objectives

Question 6

The "doctrines of lapse", which positioned princes against one another for regional thrones, gave Britain a foothold in India by

(A) allowing them to exchange a little influence at a critical time for significant influence later

(B) offering an opportunity to take over the leadership role in these areas while no one was in charge

(C) letting the British act as arbitrators in discussions between the dueling princes

(D) ensuring there were no local candidates for leadership

Question 7

From the passage, the attitude of Britain towards Indian politics can be described as:

(A) Conflicted

(B) Hypocritical

(C) Opportunistic

(D) Unbiased

Question 8

Replacement of the word despotism highlighted in the first paragraph with which of the following words would result in the LEAST change in meaning in the passage?

(A) stubborn

(B) tyranny

(C) democracy

(D) debauchery

Question 9

Which of the following sentences provides evidence that the British relied upon to justify their behavior in India to British citizens?

(A) Lines 8-10 (Thus rebellion and deposition ... civil war, occurred.)

(B) Lines 14-15 (The rationale that... their ultimate goal.)

(C) Lines 2-3 (According to ... heavy-handed folklore.)

(D) Lines 5-8 (This founder's son ... his degenerate descendants.)

Question 10

According to the passage, which of the following changes in Indian monarchies would negate the beliefs that Europeans, including the British, had about Asians in general and Indians in particular?

(A)   An impartial perception of history

(B)   A domineering and cruel monarch

(C)   A talented heir

(D)   Rebellion against tyranny

Question 11

Which of the following would best serve as an appropriate title for the given passage?

(A)   British Life in India

(B)   European Invasions and Perceptions

(C)   Controlling Stratagem of the British

(D)   The Triumph of Vigor over Tyranny

5.3 Passage 3 (The Belgian economy: from devastation to restoration)

For 200 years until World War I, French-speaking Wallonia was a technically advanced, industrial region, while Dutch-speaking Flanders was predominantly agricultural with very little
industrial work, concerned mainly with the processing of agricultural products and the making
of textiles. This disparity began to fade during the interwar period. When Belgium emerged
5 from World War II with its industrial infrastructure relatively undamaged, mainly because of
the Galopin Doctrine, the stage was set for a period of rapid development, particularly in
Flanders. The institution of the European Union and NATO in Brussels improved the state of
industry in Flanders greatly, given its proximity to Antwerp, which is the second-largest port
in Europe after Rotterdam. The older, traditional industries of Wallonia, particularly steelmak-
10 ing, began to lose their competitive edge during this period, but the general growth of world
prosperity **masked** this deterioration until the 1973 and 1979 oil price shocks and resultant
shifts in international demand sent the economy into a period of prolonged recession.

In the 1980s and 1990s, the economic center of the country continued to shift northwards to
15 Flanders. The early 1980s saw the country facing a difficult period of structural adjustment
caused by declining demand for its traditional products, deteriorating economic performance,
and neglected structural reform. Consequently, the 1980-82 recession shook Belgium to its
core—unemployment rose, social welfare costs increased, personal debt soared, the government deficit climbed to 13% of GDP, and the national debt, although mostly held domestically,
20 mushroomed. Against this grim backdrop, in 1982, Prime Minister Martens' center-right coali-
tion government formulated an economic recovery program to promote export-led growth by
enhancing the competitiveness of Belgium's export industries through an 8.5% devaluation.
Economic growth rose from 2% in 1984 to a peak of 4% in 1989. In May 1990, the government linked the franc to the German mark, primarily through closely tracking German interest
25 rates. Consequently, as German interest rates rose after 1990, Belgian rates increased and
contributed to a decline in the economic growth rate.

Although Belgium is a wealthy country, it overspent income and under-collected taxes for
years. The Belgian government reacted to the 1973 and 1979 oil price hikes with poor macroe-
30 conomic policies: it transferred workers made redundant in the private sector to the public
sector and subsidized ailing industries—coal, steel, textiles, glass, and shipbuilding—in order
to **prop** up the economy. As a result, cumulative government debt reached 121% of GNP by
the end of the 1980s *(versus a cumulative U.S. federal public debt/GNP ratio of 31.2% in 1990)*.
However, thanks to Belgium's high personal savings rate, the Belgian Government managed to
35 finance the deficit mainly from domestic savings. This minimized the deleterious effects on
the overall economy.

The economy of Belgium is varied and cannot be understood without taking the regional differences into account. Indeed, Flemish and Walloon economies differ in many respects. In
40 general, productivity in Flanders is roughly 20% higher per inhabitant than in Wallonia. Brussels' GDP per capita is much higher than either region, although this is in many ways artificial,
as many of those that work in the Brussels-Capital Region live in Flanders or Wallonia. Their
output is counted in Brussels and not where they live, artificially raising the per capita GDP
of Brussels and slightly lowering that of Flanders and Wallonia. Unemployment has remained
45 consistently more than twice as high in Wallonia than in Flanders, and even more in Brussels,
during most of the last 20 years.

Question 1

An appropriate title for this passage might be:

(A)   The Rise of Flanders to domestic leadership

(B)   Managing the challenge of structural adjustment in the post-war Belgian economy

(C)   Fiscal rally: how P.M. Martens found his legs

(D)   Which way: fickle government starves a state with too many choices

Question 2

The information in the beginning of the passage concerning the rise of Flanders over Wallonia serves to

(A)   foreshadow the counterpoint between successful and unsuccessful policy-making

(B)   introduce and demonstrate the idea of a compositional sea-change in the greater Belgian economy

(C)   show how runaway development was ready to take hold of the Belgian economy before it was mismanaged and eventually recouped

(D)   provide the reader with the factor responsible for driving away development in the greater Belgian economy

Question 3

The oil price hikes of the 1970's can be most accurately considered:

(A)   a structural problem in the Belgian economy

(B)   a pivotal turning point leading to an immediate improvement in economic policymaking

(C)   comparable to the story in which the child tells the emperor that he has no clothes

(D)   an unpredictable stroke of bad luck reversing Belgian economic momentum

Question 4

The phrase "against this grim backdrop" is used in line 20 by the author to

(A)   make light of Martens' genuine but misspent efforts to turn around the economy

(B)   show that Martens brought real change in the face of formidable challenge

(C)   pardon Martens by showing that even the most expert of handlers could not have changed the hand Belgium was dealt

(D)   imply that there was no hope for Belgium

Question 5

The genre of the passage can be categorized as:

(A)   historical

(B)   polemical

(C)   argumentative

(D)   encyclopedic

Question 6

In the passage, the author's use of the phrase "poor economic policies" and the word `prop` in paragraph 3 regarding government subsidies suggests what about his opinion of government intervention in the economy?

(A)   The government should not intervene in economic issues that can be handled privately.

(B)   The government should not support industries that are ailing.

(C)   The government must be more decisive in its decision-making.

(D)   The government cannot avoid being at the mercy of market fluctuations.

Question 7

The author's critical portrayal of the Belgian government's reactions to the oil crises in the 1970's does not necessarily make its officials economically malfeasant because:

(A)   economists are academics; politicians are pragmatists

(B)   this economic review of the Belgian economy is retrospective; the decisions made at the time were without the benefit of hindsight

(C)   there are no right or wrong answers in economics

(D)   administrators were giving the public what they wanted

Question 8

In the end of paragraph 2, the author notes that linking the franc with the German mark raised interest rates in the Belgian economy, setting off a decline in the rate of growth. However, in the last sentence of the paragraph 3, the passage states that abundant personal savings made it possible for Belgium to pay off its debts.

If higher interest rates lead to higher personal savings from which debts can be paid off, what is the best way to describe the tone of the passage regarding high interest rates?

(A)   ambivalent

(B)   foreboding

(C)   accepting

(D)   defeatist

Question 9

Replacement of the word █masked█ highlighted in the first paragraph with which of the following words would result in the LEAST change in meaning in the passage?

(A) concealed

(B) eluded

(C) deceived

(D) perplexed

Question 10

Which of the following sentences furnishes evidence for the statement explaining Flanders' climb over Wallonia?

(A) Lines 1-3 (For 200 years until ... of textiles)

(B) Line 3-4 (This disparity ... interwar period)

(C) Lines 6-9 (The institution of ... after Rotterdam)

(D) Lines 9-12 (The older, traditional ... prolonged recession)

Question 11

Which of the following measures, if true, would reduce Brussels' GDP, according to the information in the passage?

(A) calculating GDP based on number of people who work in Brussels

(B) calculating GDP based on the ways Flanders and Wallonia do it.

(C) calculating GDP based on number of people who work in Flanders and Wallonia

(D) calculating GDP based on people's place of residence

5.4   Passage 4 (Craving for fast food: whom to blame: behavior or the brain?)

Studies show that obesity is increasing rapidly, as shown in the graph below. Recent evidence from scientists has shown that eating "fast food" can be addictive in much the same way as using controlled substances can be. According to researchers, "fast food" such as hamburgers, processed sugar, and a wide range of deep fried foods can trigger a dependency in the brain
5   that perpetuates a habit of further use. It is a view that is increasingly supported by scientists who see a co-dependency between people's decisions and environmental influences (including the wide availability of "fast foods") that have structural effects on human development. The proposed conclusions contend that the brains of overeaters experience chemical changes in response to unbalanced diets with a high content of processed sugar, salt, and saturated fats.
10

In time and in some cases, if people continue a pattern of consumption containing too much unhealthy food, their intake of this food will initiate changes in the brain that elevate the minimum level of ingestion the brain needs for satiation. Moreover, since high consumption of "fast foods" stimulates opiates in the brain (substances which act as natural pain relievers),
15   large, recurrent doses of "fast food" can mimic the effects of opiates, albeit in a less intense form. Scientists raising rats on a diet of twenty-five percent sugar found that upon suddenly eliminating glucose from the rats' food supply, the animals experienced all the symptoms of withdrawal attributed to reducing traditional addictive opiates, including shivering and chattering teeth. Later, by treating rats with drugs that block opiate receptors, scientists were able
20   to lower the amount of dopamine in the nucleus acumen of rats' brains, an area linked with the dynamics of reward. Such neurochemistry can be seen in heroin addicts coping with withdrawal. By this reasoning, obesity, like other addictions, can be viewed as a disease beyond the control of those afflicted by it.

25   This has brought lawyers to argue that civil society has a responsibility to regulate food and educate people about the abuse of "unhealthy foods" in a way that is comparable to society's control of opiates and narcotics. Corporations that target this vulnerability in human beings can then be held liable for the sicknesses that result from the poor eating habits overwhelming their customers. Still, some scientists scoff at the lengths to which their colleagues seek to
30   separate the decision making process from people's behavior. For these researchers, the distinction between a habit and an addiction is not quantitative, but qualitative. Their consensus is that individuals can still moderate their behavior to control the effects of what they eat on their systems.

35   However, what the latter fail to take into account is that the obesity epidemic clearly suggests that seemingly personal choices are not personal anymore; they have already been decided. The obesity epidemic and the problems with overeating don't have much to do with people overeating fruits or healthy foods, but with excess consumption of sugars and fats, since sugar and fats have become extremely cheap to produce on a mass-scale. Such deep preva-
40   lence and ubiquitous presence outweighs any other choice, influencing the decisions and thus the decision-making power of the gullible public. More and more studies prove that industrial, sugar-, fat- and salt-laden food, food that is made in plants rather than grown from a plant, is biologically addictive. The "just say no" approach did not work in drug addiction and would not work for food addiction either.

45
The problem with emphasizing personal or social responsibility is that it will take the onus off the government or the industry, leaving the hapless public facing the epidemic. The focus shifts away from environmental factors such as advertising and lack of menu labelling, as well as from the addictive properties of industrial food, factors which override normal biological

50
or psychological control mechanisms. Even from an economic perspective, government intervention is necessary, as is always the case when the market fails to provide the optimum amount of good for society's well-being. To bring about effective and sustainable change, it will take more than just policy change. It will require a change in perceptions, environment, and support mechanisms to reverse the trend.

Question 1

The passage seems to suggest that scientists who see a co-dependence between people's decisions and environmental influences would affirm that

(A) human decision-making has unconscious, chemical influences

(B) overeaters are not responsible for their behavior with their eating disorders

(C) obesity is a public health crisis

(D) overeaters continue to eat because they are unable to overcome the difficulties of withdrawal

Question 2

Based on the information provided in the passage, the relationship between administering drugs that block opiate receptors and dopamine levels can be considered:

(A) dependent

(B) directly correlated

(C) related

(D) unrelated

Question 3

Lawyers defending corporations against the findings of researchers on the effects of "fast food" would most likely argue that

(A) obesity is a pre-existing condition in individuals

(B) obese people must treat their disease with medication that blocks opiate receptors

(C) the distinction between a habit and an addiction is "not quantitative but qualitative"

(D) corporations were not aware that "fast food" caused chemical dependency because the science confirming it is so new

Question 4

By labeling obesity as a disease, the scientists in the passage seek to point out that

(A) the obese need to obey a strict diet

(B) the obese are more vulnerable to the health hazards of chronic consumption of "fast food" than those who are not obese

(C) obesity is a result of factors that cannot be understood solely as the result of the behavior of individuals

(D) obesity exists in an individual whether or not they overeat

Question 5

Some scientists in the passage who dispute the conclusions of their colleagues who link obesity with chemical factors find fault with their colleagues'

(A) findings

(B) expertise

(C) assumptions

(D) methodology

Question 6

The phrasing of dissenting scientists that notes "the distinction between habit and addiction is not quantitative but qualitative" in line 56 objects to the assumption

(A) that linking a chemical process to a behavioral pattern is sufficient to categorize someone as diseased

(B) that there is only one factor which determines a person's behavior

(C) that differences in behavior or choices do not contribute at all to eventual addiction and possible neurochemistry changes

(D) that any amount of fast food is bad for people

Question 7

From the passage, the role of dopamine in the rats' brains seems to

(A) reduce food intake

(B) block opiates

(C) punish rats when opiates are received

(D) instruct the rat to eat more

Question 8

As presented in the passage, lawyers who would seek to take "fast food" restaurants to court for damaging public health would agree with which of the following?

(A)   the government is not knowledgeable enough to safeguard public health

(B)   corporations are responsible for the consequences of their products

(C)   the responsibility to determine what a good product is should be determined by the market

(D)   people should take responsibility for their own diets

Question 9

Which of the following, if true, would strengthen the argument made in the fourth paragraph?

(A)   Obese people make better food choices when surrounded by healthy options.

(B)   Obese people always feel depressed when they are dieting.

(C)   Obese people can successfully lose weight and keep it off for the rest of their lives.

(D)   Exercising more and consuming fewer calories can reduce weight dramatically.

The following graph shows the rate of obesity in adults and the rate of being overweight in both children and adults in the United States from 1960 - 2004.

The following two questions are based on the graph.

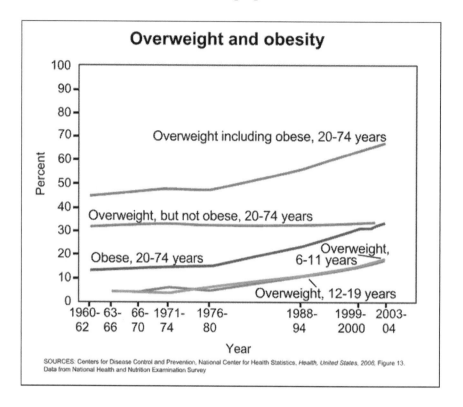

Question 10

All of the following statements are supported by the graph, EXCEPT.

(A) Post 1980, for the age group 20-74, the percentage of those who are overweight, but not obese, has risen significantly.

(B) Post 1980, for the age group 6-19, the percentage of those who are overweight has risen significantly.

(C) For the age group 20-74, from 1960-80, the percentage of those who are obese did not increase as significantly as it did from 1960-2004.

(D) From 1988 onward, for the age groups 6-11 and 12-19, the increase in the percentage of those who are overweight is almost the same.

Question 11

Which of following statements is supported by the graph?

(A) Youngsters are relatively less overweight than adults.

(B) At any time period in the US, in the age-group 20-74, there are at least 50% of people who are overweight, but not obese.

(C) If we plot a line graph for those who are overweight, but not obese, for the age group 30-50 (not given in the graph), it will lie exactly on the line graph for those who are overweight, but not obese, for the age group 20-74.

(D) From 1988 onward, for the age groups 6-11 and 12-19, the percentage of those who are obese is almost the same.

5.5 Passage 5 (Gas attacks during the World Wars)

WWI introduced the scariest attack weapon – poison gas. It was ruthless, and random. It could be used even when actual fighting was not going on. The machine guns wounded and killed far more soldiers, but soldiers could seek shelter from guns in the trenches, and even if they did not, death was instant, whereas poison gas caught soldiers unawares and death was slow and
5 excruciatingly painful, dragging on for days with no relief until it sapped the courage of people around the afflicted. Gas usage had been considered uncivilized, but the French resorted to its usage in August 1914 in an attempt to rout the Germans. Unfortunately, the Germans were the first to give gas warfare serious development and it became used extensively before the war was over. See the info-graphic presented below for details of the specific gases employed,
10 and the effects of those gases.

The attack on Pearl Harbor by the Japanese introduced America to the world theater of World War II. What was unique about this battle was that American citizens experienced it as the first attack on American soil in what was then recent memory. Throughout World War I, Americans
15 mostly felt secure in their homes. However, the changing times and the audacity of national-istic world powers raised questions as to the need for civilian defense. The highest priority was the protection of children from possible attack. The escalation of World War II already involved lengthy campaigns of civil terror waged by opposing powers. No power with a sol-diering part in the war was immune or blameless. Germany unleashed the lengthiest bombing
20 campaign of the war on the people of London primarily to weaken British morale. Later, the Allied Forces would fire bomb the German city of Dresden. Dresden housed an almost entirely civilian population and had incidental wartime production.

Early on, Britain and the United States enacted an emergency measure to protect their youth
25 population. A leading concern was the exposure to gas attacks, an effective measure against unwitting urban dwellers. Immediately after Pearl Harbor, thousands of military training masks were rushed to people living on the islands. However, the available equipment was unsuitable for protecting children. Instead, Hawaiian officials produced an **expedient** made up of bunny ears and a hood. This would lead to further improvisation in the protection of the
30 child civilian population. The Sun Rubber Company designed a mask based on the universal Walt Disney cartoon figure Mickey Mouse. The Mickey Mouse gas mask was then approved by the Chemical Warfare Service of the U.S. Department of Defense, with the assumption that other winning designs could follow the success of this first run. The popularity of these masks was dependent on internalizing their use in children by making their presence part of a per-
35 ceived game. This potentially reduced the element of fear that the masks conveyed on their recipients. If the element of fear could be diminished, gas masks might be employed by their owners more quickly in the event of an attack, and also worn without interruption.

All of this would increase the chances of survival of the youth population, of no small concern
40 to a nation with large numbers of its working age males facing the perils of combat overseas.

By the time the war ended, the main user of poison gas was Germany, followed by France and then Britain. Though poison gas was a terrifying weapon, its actual impact, rather like the tank, is open to debate. The number of fatalities was relatively few - even if the terror impact
45 did not diminish for the duration of the war.

The British army (including the British Empire) had 188,000 gas casualties, but only 8,100 fatalities amongst them. It is believed that the nation that suffered the most fatalities was Russia (over 50,000 men), while France had 8,000 fatalities. In total there were about 1,250,000
50 gas casualties in the war, but only 91,000 fatalities (less than 10%) with over 50% of these fatalities being Russian. However, these figures do not take into account the number of men who died from poison gas related injuries years after the end of the war; nor do they take into account the number of men who survived but were so badly incapacitated by poison gas that they could hold down no job once they had been released by the army.

Question 1

According to the passage, the main distinction between World War I and World War II for Americans was:

(A) the lengthy campaigns of civil terror

(B) the blame shared by all participating powers

(C) the mobilization of civilian factories for military use

(D) the first violation of national security in several generations

Question 2

The purpose of national armies engaging in civil terror is presented by the passage

(A) to destroy the civilian wartime infrastructure

(B) to reduce the number of potential reinforcements for dwindling armies

(C) to keep armies and pilots active during long periods without confrontation

(D) to destroy the enemy's willingness to continue fighting

Question 3

The design of gas masks to look like a cartoon character was intended to

(A) make the war seem less omnipresent to children

(B) make children less afraid of a foreign attack

(C) induce children to learn how to use the mask properly

(D) bring a level of normalcy back to everyday life

Question 4

The passage observes that the special efforts taken to consider the need to protect the youth population were based on concerns that

(A) they may be needed to replenish the lines of men in the trenches

(B) they would be needed to repopulate the country if the men overseas did not return

(C) they may have been the only ones available to work jobs throughout the economy after the war

(D) they were the main concern of parents who vote

Question 5

In paragraph 3, the word `expedient` most nearly means:

(A) a dire consequence

(B) a cleaning agent

(C) a response to an urgent need

(D) a terror tactic

Question 6

The benefit of internalizing the use of these masks in children was that

(A) they would wear them to bed

(B) they would take the masks to school

(C) they would encourage friends to use them

(D) they would lack fear upon wearing them

Question 7

It can be inferred from the passage that a significant avoidable danger of a wartime terror attack is:

(A) the youth of the civilian population

(B) poor decision making on the part of unprepared civilians

(C) plunging civilian morale

(D) lack of warning of an attack

Question 8

Which of the following sentences provides evidence for the claim that attack from poison gas was more feared than any other attack?

(A) Line 1 (WWI introduced ... poison gas.)

(B) Lines 1-2 (It was ... going on)

(C) Lines 55-59 (However, these ... by the army)

(D) Lines 2-6 (The machines guns ... . around the afflicted)

Question 9

According to the information contained in the final two paragraphs, which of the following conclusions are supported?

(A) Poison gas had far more fatalities in WWI than did any other warfare tactic.

(B) The impact of tanks in a war is negligible.

(C) Poison gas impacted far more than 1,250,000 people.

(D) Germany, France, and Britain should not have used poison gas.

The following two questions are based on the following info-graphic.

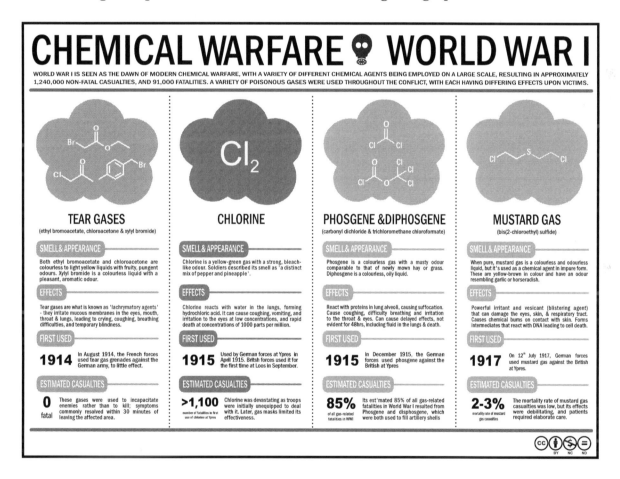

The above info-graphic shows the details on the gases employed in WWI as part of chemical warfare.

Question 10

According to the details presented above, which of the above gases would a person have been least aware of, but was fatal?

(A) Tear gas

(B) Chlorine gas

(C) Phosgene gas

(D) Impure Mustard gas

Question 11

Which of the following elements, if unavailable, will hamper the production of the maximum number of the gases?

(A) Bromine

(B) Chlorine

(C) Sulfur

(D) Oxygen

5.6   Passage 6 (Lord Dalhousie's reforms in India)

The reforms introduced by Lord Dalhousie in India during his eight-year stint as the Governor General are many. Dalhousie introduced a new system of internal communication in India. Dalhousie convinced the authorities of the need for the railways and laid down the main lines of their development. He envisaged a network of railways connecting the main places with
5 the ports, and provided both for strategical needs and commercial development. Gradually all important cities and towns were linked with railway lines. The railway lines were not built out of the Indian Exchequer but by private English Companies under a system of "Government Guarantee". Besides facilitating trade and commerce and minimizing distances, the railways have gone a long way in uniting India.

10

Furthermore, In 1852, Dalhousie introduced the Electric Telegraph System in India. The first telegraph line from Calcutta to Agra was opened in 1854, covering a distance of 800 miles. By 1857, it was extended to Lahore and Peshawar. In Burma a line was laid down from Rangoon to Mandalay. People could send messages from one place to another place very easily with
15 this telegraph system. Before Lord Dalhousie, military boards were in charge of the construction of Public Works. Hence Civilian works were completely neglected by the military board. A separate Public Works Department was established by Lord Dalhousie. Irrigational works were undertaken on an extensive scale. The construction of the Ganges Canal was completed and was inaugurated on April 8, 1854. Many bridges and canals were constructed, and the
20 construction of the Grand Trunk Road was taken up. Dalhousie's special contribution was the construction of an engineering college at Roorkee and in other presidencies.

Most importantly, Lord Dalhousie is credited with the creation of the modern postal system in India. Dalhousie, who held many roles in the administration and internal development of
25 the region, contributed to the Indian postal system by sweeping away the fabric of its past obstructions and levying a uniform rate of postage.

All letters weighing less than a prescribed amount in weight would require the same postal fee (half an anna) regardless of their destination or origin. This idea of instituting a uniform unit
30 of weight and of charge for the whole of the vast Indian empire seemed sheer folly to many orthodox financiers of his time. It was, they said, pushing Rowland Hill's scheme of a penny postage for England to an extreme. For these onlookers, Dalhousie's plan was not so much an extension of the English penny postage scheme as a **reductio ad absurdum** of the reform that had been effected in Great Britain. What could be more extravagant or more unjust than to
35 levy the same charge on two letters, one of which was to be delivered to the adjoining street, and the other to the opposite side of India?

Lord Dalhousie was not significantly deterred by the criticism. Because of the uniform rate of postage, the old wrangle over the payment for delivery of every letter, from which the rural
40 postman invariably managed to squeeze something additional for himself at the expense of the recipient, could be replaced by a simple system of postage stamps. The system was more reliable for the person mailing the letter, and encouraged increased patronage.

The proof of his success was the renewal of the postal system as a self-sustaining organization
45 rather than its continuance as a chronic drain on British colonial finances. The social results were even more important. It has been said that the half-penny post that Lord Dalhousie

put in place in India was more consequential than the telegraph, the railway, and even public instruction for reversing the isolation which predated it. One historian goes so far as to say: 'It has done more than perhaps his telegraphs or his railways, in revolutionizing the old, stagnant, and self-isolated life in India.' In the old days, the postmaster was often the station doctor, or some subaltern who had plenty of spare time on his hands; in the present day village schoolmasters are found in the remotest districts acting in the same capacity.

Question 1

The objections to the uniform postal rate in India were related to:

(A) the fact that it was not fair to charge the same rate for different degrees of service

(B) the fact that it was an unproven method

(C) the fact that it conveyed a lack of trust in postal workers

(D) the inability of the letter delivery service to handle a flood of cross-India mail

Question 2

According to the passage, the main benefit of the half-penny post scheme to India was

(A) an increase in the rate of communication throughout the subcontinent

(B) increased rates of literacy

(C) reduced corruption among the postmen

(D) its independence from British financial support

Question 3

It can be inferred from the results of Dalhousie's revisions of India's postal system that

(A) the only way to see whether something will be successful is to put it into practice

(B) if something works on a small scale, it should work on a large scale as well, if executed properly

(C) disorganization and unreliability may be more costly than charging at rates below expenses

(D) Britain's financial support of the postal system gave it no incentive to improve

Question 4

One lesson that can be taken from Dalhousie's success is that

(A) personal experience can be more informed than extensive theoretical knowledge

(B) postal systems are one example of a good that is not subject to supply and demand curves

(C) there had been British mismanagement

(D) for Britain's purposes, the penny postage scheme should have preceded the telegraph, the railway, and Public Instruction

Question 5

In the middle of the fourth paragraph, the term **reductio ad absurdum** most closely means:

(A) to misunderstand the purpose of an idea

(B) to simplify an idea while losing its key elements

(C) to extend an idea to a scale beyond which it is practical

(D) to make a functional premise seem ridiculous

Question 6

The passage specifies that simplifying the mail system compensated the post office for the costs of uniform postage by

(A) reducing staff

(B) increasing patronage

(C) increasing reliability

(D) creating a market for written communication

Question 7

The most decisive evidence of Dalhousie having made the right decision in instituting his postal scheme is

(A) increased patronage

(B) reduced corruption in India

(C) its previous success in England as Rowland Hill's postal scheme

(D) the attainment of a financially sound postal system

Question 8

The experience of Lord Dalhousie in the passage demonstrates that

(A) larger markets may experience increased transaction costs

(B) transaction costs are negligible

(C) postal workers are always corrupt

(D) standardization has the ability to reduce transaction costs

Question 9

Which of the following statements shows that the authorities were not necessarily in favor of the reforms done by Dalhousie?

(A)	Lines 1-2 (The reforms … are many)

(B)	Lines 3-4 (Dalhousie convinced … development)

(C)	Lines 16-17 (Before Lord … public works)

(D)	Lines 22-23 (Dalhousie's special … other presidencies)

Question 10

Which of the following conclusions is supported in the final sentence of the passage?

(A)	Villages do not need medical personnel with special training.

(B)	Postmasters have a lot of time since Dalhousie's reforms.

(C)	Village schoolmasters have a lot of spare time.

(D)	Doctors are not interested in taking up station in villages and rural areas.

Question 11

The author's tone towards Lord Dalhousie's work can be said to be:

(A)	qualified approval

(B)	keen esteem

(C)	veiled Reproof

(D)	disguised skepticism

5.7   Passage 7 (The sustainability of Homo sapiens)

Biomass, in ecology, is the mass of living biological organisms in a given area or ecosystem at a given time.

The positioning of human beings as one of the species with the largest biomasses on earth,
5   and as the leading influence on earth's ecosystems, is the result of the ecological processes which brought about their migration from the African savannah, and geographically dispersed them throughout the world. It can be said the most rudimentary measure of the success of the species is its position near the top of the aggregate biomass scale. Biomass is the total mass of all living members of a species. For human beings, it is a reflection of their claim on
10   territory, and their consumption of resources as a species. It might be short-sighted to belittle the success of an emerging species or breed for being small in number if it is evident that the members of the species are elegant and well-adjusted. However, the ability to adapt one's habitat to the largest ecosystem, while still retaining the flexibility to deal with local demands on the population, may be considered high art in the annals of successful adaptation. It is
15   here that human beings have had nearly unparalleled success (insects being larger in world-wide biomass). As a result, human beings exist in huge numbers. It is a fact that human beings have remained in a generally undifferentiated form that allows them to rank highly as a single successful species.

20   The whole world has been tenanted with life. Human beings are considered unique, as they retain their form as they travel from environment to environment. Historically, human beings, like all organisms, may be driven into new areas, or a new environment may spring up around them as a result of drought, competition, or geological changes.

25   Still, human beings have been able to adjust their behavior sufficiently to avoid having nature make such extensive piecemeal adjustments to them that entirely distinct workable alternatives of the same model occupy the new space. It was through such piecemeal adjustments that dinosaurs yielded to pigeons, primitive fish to amphibians and then eventually to whales, and even Homo sapiens partially to Neanderthals for a time.

30
What normally happens when ecological processes interfere is that species usually get geo-graphically isolated. Geological processes can fragment a population through such events as the emergence of mountain ranges, canyon formation, glacial processes, the formation or de-struction of land bridges, or the subsidence of large bodies of water. On a global scale, plate
35   tectonics are major geological factors leading to separation of populations and the result-ing distribution of species. The separated populations then undergo genotypic or phenotypic divergence as they become subjected to different selective pressures; they independently un-dergo genetic drift; and different mutations arise in the gene pools of the populations. The separate populations over time may evolve distinctly different characteristics. If the geograph-
40   ical barriers are later removed, members of the two populations may be unable to successfully mate with each other, at which point the genetically isolated groups have emerged as a differ-ent species.

In all cases, these offshoots and also-rans of each species had to co-exist alongside their pre-
45   ceding heritage. Thus, it can be said that many species, through one of their members, were able to succeed in carrying the genetic information of the group into another ecosystem. But

eventually, each derivation became classified as something other than its ancestor. In this way, the transfer of genetic material circles the globe, and a species takes on scientifically unique identities at different times and in different places. Humans thus remain distinct, not because
50   they are the first to exist in so many habitats and take advantage of so many resources, but in that they have become one of the relatively few organisms to accomplish widespread popula- tion of different habitats while being able to exchange genetic material with others from their group, even if they had been largely geographically isolated over many generations. Thus, hu- man beings are so marvelously successful as a species because despite separation, evolution
55   did not result in changes drastic enough to reproductively isolate separated humans.

Question 1

According to the passage, the high ranking of human beings on a planetary biomass scale directly demonstrates which aspects of their success?

(A)   their position at the top of the food chain

(B)   their ability to eat almost anything and engineer their environment

(C)   their consumption of resources and claim on territory

(D)   their mobility

Question 2

What makes human beings unique in their colonization of the Earth is that:

(A)   genetically they followed a similar path to that of dinosaurs

(B)   they withstood dispersal while becoming the only surviving species in their genus

(C)   they are the highest ranked organisms on the biomass scale

(D)   they carried their genetic code to all parts of the world

Question 3

According to the passage, what characteristic has allowed human beings to avoid splitting into different species?

(A)   their ability to reproduce with all the members of their species

(B)   minimal exposure to geographic isolation

(C)   their ability to adjust their behavior to fit their environment

(D)   the presence of a very diverse genetic code with many permutations in a large population

Question 4

The passage quantifies success of any species in terms of:

(A)   the population density of a species

(B)   the population size of a species

(C)   the global dispersion of its genetic code

(D)   the degree of adaptation to its environment

Question 5

According to the passage, an important factor in the success of a species is:

(A)   geographic dispersion

(B)   the age of the preceding species

(C)   mutation

(D)   sexual selection

Question 6

The passage discusses genetic material in regard to which of the following:

(A)   consumable resources

(B)   mutations of genes

(C)   spiral forms of genes

(D)   migration of species

Question 7

The style of the passage may be considered:

(A)   biased

(B)   polemical

(C)   balanced

(D)   vague

Question 8

Which of the following sentences provides evidence to explain the success of human beings on earth?

(A)   Lines 1-2 (Biomass, ... a given time)

(B)   Lines 13-15 (However, the ability ... successful adaptation)

(C)   Lines 55-58 (Thus, human ... separated humans)

(D)   Lines 17 (As a result human beings exist in huge numbers.)

Question 9

Which of the following would be the most appropriate as the tone of the author towards the success of human beings on earth?

(A)   capricious endorsement

(B)   sharp disparagement

(C)   absolute neutrality

(D)   tentative approbation

The following two questions are based on the following graph.

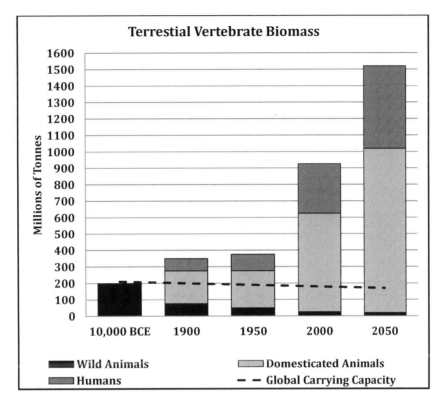

Question 10

The greatest percentage increase in the biomass of humans has occurred in which of the following periods?

(A) 1900-1950

(B) 1950-2000

(C) 2000-2050

(D) 1900-1950 and 2000-2050

Question 11

Which of the following deductions is supported by the graph?

(A) While the biomass of wild animals and that of domesticated animals have been decreasing, that of humans has been increasing.

(B) While the biomass of wild animals and that of humans have been decreasing, that of domesticated animals has been increasing.

(C) While the biomass of wild animals has been decreasing, that of domesticated animals and that of humans have been increasing.

(D) While the biomass of domesticated animals has been decreasing, that of wild animals and that of humans have been increasing.

5.8 Passage 8 (The Influence of the British Poetry of World War One)

Perhaps the most persistent myth about the British poetry of World War One is that it became
progressively more realistic as soldier-poets learned more about the horrors of modern trench
warfare. According to this orthodoxy, the pastoral patriotism of Brooke soon gave way, in
the mud and blood of Flanders, to the angry realism of Sassoon and Owen. Thus when we
5 think of World War One poetry today, the poems that instantly come to the minds of most
readers are those angry and satirical anti-war poems, such as Sassoon's "Base Details" and
"Blighters" and Owen's "Dulce et decorum est," the last being probably the most famous, or
certainly the most widely anthologized, poem of the war. The problem with this view is that it
is based on a relatively small group of poems that, despite their indisputable excellence, are in
10 many ways atypical of the bulk of poetry, including much of the good poetry, written during
the war. That poetry was deeply indebted to the nineteenth-century poetic tradition running
from Wordsworth and the Romantics through the major Victorian poets to Hardy and beyond.
The majority of the war poets worked within this tradition to produce, as has been recently
argued, the trench lyric. But it is not just much of the poetry of World War One that belongs
15 to this tradition. The last two paragraphs of what many regard as one of the best memoirs
to come out of the war, Siegfried Sassoon's "Memoirs of a Fox-Hunting Man" (1928), emerge
from the same tradition and constitute a prose version of the trench lyric composed by the
solider-poets.

20 At first glance, a work by the author of some of the bitterest and most angry anti-war poems
of World War One may seem an unlikely place to observe the conventions of Romantic poetry,
but the ending of "Memoirs of a Fox-Hunting Man" reveals just how insistently the Romantic
lyric imposed its form and structure on the imaginations of the writers of World War One.
Readers have consistently noted how the language of the last two paragraphs of "Memoirs
25 of a Fox-Hunting Man" self-consciously echoes Thomas Hardy's "The Darkling Thrush." But
it is not just a single poem by Hardy that lies behind the end of "Memoirs of a Fox-Hunting
Man". Sassoon is doing more than including an oblique reference to a specific poem. Both
Hardy's lyric and the ending of Sassoon's fictional memoir belong to a structurally identifiable
Romantic and Victorian lyric genre running from the early Wordsworth and Coleridge to such
30 late nineteenth-century incarnations as Hardy's lyric and on into the twentieth century. By
imitating this form of the Romantic and post-Romantic lyric, Sassoon is aligning himself with
a tradition of English poetry and a particular lyric form more than a century old. So strongly
had this genre enforced itself upon the literary consciousness of poets and readers alike that,
by the end of the nineteenth century, it had become virtually synonymous with the lyric poem.
35 The soldier-poets of the Great War carried this model with them in their minds and in their
copies of The Oxford Book of English Verse into the trenches of France and Flanders, along
with their rifles, their kitbags, and (before long) their gas masks.

Sassoon, like Rosenberg, does not abandon a set of worn-out poetic conventions so he can write
40 directly and realistically, and hence originally, about it. Rather he translates a pre-existing
model into local terms. Even literary memoirists, who are expected to respect the facts, can
only be as realistic as the artificial literary conventions available to them will allow them to
be. Writers write realistically not by directly "telling it like it is," but by telling it like it's told
in literature. They must, as Northrop Frye told us half a century ago, find, or adapt, a set of
45 literary conventions, and out of this old paradigm create a new literary form , and he famously
states "Poetry is made out of other poems".

Question 1

The author is mainly concerned with

(A) repudiating a historical misconception

(B) discussing the different aspects of the great British poets of the war era

(C) highlighting the importance of nineteenth century Romantics and Victorian poets

(D) establishing that new paradigms in literature are not created through existing conventions

Question 2

With which of the following options is the author most likely to agree?

(A) that the most famous poem of the war is an archetype of the bulk of the war poetry

(B) that prose written during the war is inspired by nineteenth century poetic tradition

(C) that poetry grew a more and more realistic new style as soldiers got into modern warfare

(D) that Sassoon influenced most of the poets and writers of the British war era

Question 3

Which of the following options presents the author's reasons for believing that World War One poetry did not become more realistic and evolve into a different literary form?

(A) The bulk of the poems written during the time the war poets worked was within the nineteenth century poetic tradition to produce literary conventions of the trench lyric.

(B) Pastoral patriotism soon gave way, in the mud and blood of Flanders, to the angry realism of war poets, which led to the formation of the trench lyric.

(C) Writers write realistically by abandoning conventions, not by adapting them in literature and sticking to literary conventions.

(D) Northrop Frye mentions the adaptation of literary conventions.

Question 4

In the passage, the highlighted phrase **That poetry** refers to

(A) Sassoon's "Base Details" and "Blighters", and Owen's "Dulce et decorum est"

(B) Poetry written by Wordsworth, the Romantics, and the major Victorian poets

(C) Angry and satirical anti-war poems

(D) The bulk of poetry written during the War

Question 5

According to the context of the passage, which of the following can serve as the closest alternative to the highlighted word pastoral ?

(A)   serene

(B)   realistic

(C)   divine

(D)   satirical

Question 6

In which of the following sentences of the passage does the author demonstrate that Sassoon's work "Memoirs of a Fox-Hunting Man" is in keeping with the nineteenth century poetic tradition of the Romantics and Victorian poets?

(A)   Lines 42-43: "Sassoon, like Rosenberg, does not ... and hence originally, about it"

(B)   Lines 16-19: "The last two paragraphs of what many ... composed by the solider-poets"

(C)   Lines 21-25: "At first glance, a work by the ... the writers of World War One"

(D)   Lines 12-14: "That poetry was ... and beyond"

Question 7

Which of the following best describe the author's attitude towards the view that increasingly modern warfare rendered poetry of the war more and more angry and sarcastic?

(A)   qualified enthusiasm

(B)   utter disgust

(C)   healthy regard

(D)   cautious dubiety

Question 8

Which of the following conclusions can be drawn from the final quote made by Northrop Frye?

(A)   New poetry is different from earlier poetry.

(B)   Sassoon has plagiarized Hardy's poetry.

(C)   All poems have been influenced by earlier poetry.

(D)   No poetry can contain any new idea.

Question 9

Which of the following sentences provides an answer for why solider-poets wrote trench lyrics in the nineteenth-century poetic tradition?

(A) Lines 25-27: "Readers have ... Hardy's "The Darkling Thrush.""

(B) Lines 34-37: "So strongly ... the lyric poem"

(C) Lines 29-32: "Both Hardy's ... twentieth century"

(D) Lines 28-29: "Sassoon is ... a specific poem"

Question 10

It can be inferred from the passage that the tone of Sassoon's poetry was most similar to poetry of

(A) Brooke

(B) Owen

(C) Hardy

(D) Frye

Question 11

Which of the following scenarios is most similar to the situation of Sassoon's writing?

(A) A biologist creates a new system of classification based on the existing taxonomic system.

(B) A manufacturer starts a completely new product line to add to his existing product lines.

(C) A researcher creates a new method of annotations unlike any other made yet.

(D) A musician selects a theme and creates a very melodious song.

5.9   Passage 9 (New evidence clears up a long puzzle)

The earliest accumulation of oxygen in the atmosphere is arguably the most important biological event in Earth history. The general consensus asserts that appreciable oxygen first accumulated in Earth's atmosphere around 2.3 billion years ago during the so-called Great Oxidation Event (GOE). Scientists have long speculated as to why animal species didn't **burgeon**
5 sooner, even though plants had long started appearing and developing, once sufficient oxygen covered the Earth's surface. Animals first appeared and began to prosper at the end of the Proterozoic period, about 600 to 700 million years ago—but in the billion-year stretch before that, when there was also plenty of oxygen, there were no animals.

10 Evidently, the air was not oxygen-rich enough then. The oxygen levels during the billion or more years before the rise of animals were only 0.1 percent of what they are today. In other words, Earth's atmosphere couldn't have supported a diversity of creatures, no matter what genetic advancements were in place. While there is no question that genetic and ecological innovations are ultimately behind the rise of animals, there is also no question that for animal
15 life to flourish, a certain level of oxygen is required. The evidence was found by analyzing chromium isotopes in ancient sediments from China, Australia, Canada, and the United States. Chromium is found in the Earth's continental crust, and chromium oxidation, the process recorded by the chromium isotopes, is directly linked to the presence of free oxygen in the atmosphere. Specifically, samples deposited in shallow, iron-rich ocean areas near the ancient
20 shoreline were studied and compared with other samples deposited in similar settings but taken from younger shoreline locales that were known to have higher levels of oxygen.

The question about the role of oxygen in controlling the first appearance of animal has long vexed scientists. Previous estimates, which put the oxygen level at 40 percent of today's condi-
25 tions during pre-animal times, were based on very loose constraints, leaving open the possibility that oxygen was already sufficiently high to support animal life, and shifting the absence of animal life before the end of the Proterozoic to other controls. Oxygen levels were highly dynamic in the early atmosphere, with the potential for occasional spikes. However, it also seems clear that there are first-order differences in the nature of Earth's surface chromium cycling
30 before the rise of animals versus the time interval coincident with their first appearance—implying very small oxygen conditions before. These differences are recorded in a dramatic shift in the chromium isotope data, with clear signals of cycling beneath a more oxygen-rich atmosphere at the time the animals appear.

35 The late Proterozoic—the time period beginning less than a billion years ago following this remarkable chapter of sustained low levels of oxygen—was strikingly different, marked by extreme climatic events manifested in global-scale glaciation, indications of at least intervals of modern-like oxygen abundances, and the emergence and diversification of the earliest animals. Oxygen played a major if not dominant role in the timing of that rise and, in particular, in
40 the subsequent emergence of complex ecologies for animal life on and within the sediment, predator-prey relationships, and large bodies.

Question 1

Which of the following provides the most accurate inference implied by the new evidence?

(A) Animal species flourished sooner than is believed by scientists.

(B) There was plenty of free oxygen before the end of the Proterozoic period.

(C) The evidence from Canada and the US proves the existence of chromium cycles in the Proterozoic period.

(D) Before the end of the Proterozoic period, the atmosphere contained much less oxygen than had been estimated.

Question 2

Which of the following, if true, would weaken the claim made in the final paragraph?

(A) Chromium oxidation is the only reliable indicator of oxygen levels.

(B) Oxygen levels required to sustain animal life are far higher than currently believed.

(C) Chromium samples from other continents match the samples from Australia.

(D) Shoreline locales are not quite representative of the rest of the landforms.

Question 3

Which of the following best describes the role of the second paragraph in the whole passage?

(A) elaborating on the contents of the first paragraph

(B) buttressing the claim in the previous paragraph

(C) detailing an alternative explanation

(D) offsetting the theory of the first paragraph

Question 4

Which of the following explains the chief concern of the passage?

(A) discussing a scientific phenomenon

(B) explaining the origin of life

(C) supporting an original hypothesis

(D) revealing new evidence

Question 5

Which of the following was believed to be true by scientists?

(A)   The oxygen level was 40 percent of what it is today.

(B)   Animals first appeared 600 to 700 million years ago.

(C)   The oxygen level influenced the appearance of animals.

(D)   For animal life to flourish, a certain level of oxygen is not required.

Question 6

According to the passage, which of the following statements is still considered true?

(A)   Oxygen is not necessary for animals to prosper.

(B)   Oxygen levels were relatively stable in the early atmosphere.

(C)   The atmosphere contained plenty of oxygen around the time animals appeared.

(D)   Early oxygen levels were high enough to support animals.

Question 7

Which of the following would perfectly replace the highlighted word burgeon as used in the context of the passage?

(A)   flourish

(B)   dwindle

(C)   wane

(D)   evolve

Question 8

Which of the following best describes the tone of the scientists towards the Great Oxidation Event and the rise of animal species before the evidence from chromium data?

(A)   exasperated

(B)   disgusted

(C)   cognizant

(D)   elated

Question 9

Which paragraph provides evidence that clears up the long standing puzzle about the rise and development of animal species?

(A)   the first paragraph

(B)   the second paragraph

(C)   the third paragraph

(D)   the final paragraph

The following two questions are based on the following graph.

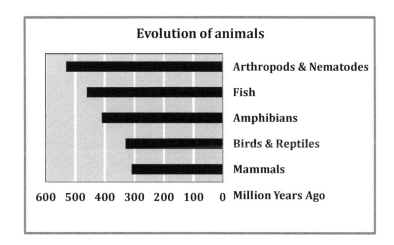

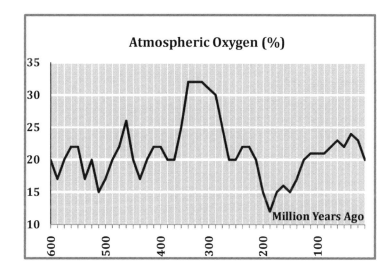

Question 10

Which of the following deductions is supported by the passage and the graphs?

(A) Before 600 million years ago, there was hardly any oxygen on Earth.

(B) Before 600 million years ago, no living organism existed on Earth.

(C) Before 600 million years ago, oxygen level must have been less than 20% on Earth.

(D) Before 600 million years ago, the air was not oxygen-rich enough on Earth.

Question 11

Which of the following deductions is supported by the graphs?

(A) All five categories for animals (Arthropods & Nematodes through Mammals) had evolved once the oxygen level reached 25% for the first time on Earth.

(B) All five categories for animals (Arthropods & Nematodes through Mammals) had evolved once the oxygen level was at its maximum percentage level on Earth.

(C) At least two categories of animals among Arthropods & Nematodes through Mammals had evolved once the oxygen level reached 20% for the first time on Earth.

(D) At least four categories of animals among Arthropods & Nematodes through Mammals had evolved once the oxygen level reached 25% for the second time on the earth.

5.10   Passage 10: Paired passage (BRICS economies)

Passage 1 (Mike, Chief Economist, on BRICS countries)

The notion that the era of emerging BRICS countries is over, and that among them only China would make it to the group of high-income countries, is outlandish. No doubt the growth rates in the BRICS group of Brazil, Russia, India, China, and South Africa have been hit by the global slowdown, and countries like India further singed by capital flow reversals. But this is
5   a temporary phenomenon that will peter out sooner rather than later. BRICS economies are bound to reinvent the global economic order, and even fashion it in their own image, once the macroeconomic balances are restored and foreign investment flows rebound, boosted by reforms.

10   Similarly, the argument that the rest of the BRICS countries will fall by the wayside while China continues to march ahead is flawed. Not only has China's growth rate almost halved from peak levels, it's in fact facing a double whammy with its export-led economy badly hit by the slowdown in advanced country markets – as rising wages and a shortage of skills erode its competitive base even as it struggles to shift over to a domestic consumption-based growth
15   model. This will probably help other BRICS countries like India to make new inroads into the global markets for manufactured goods and close in fast on China.

In fact, the most recent trends in the global Greenfield investments, which exclude mergers and acquisitions, validate this argument. The numbers show that while new FDI (Foreign Di-
20   rect Investment) projects to China have come down sharply by almost half after the global slowdown, other BRICS countries haven't been so badly bruised. On the contrary, the gap be-tween China and other BRICS countries has in fact shrunk, with India accounting for 30% of the Greenfield FDI projects in BRICS as compared to the 40% share of China.

Passage 2 (Dr. Walter, Professor, on BRICS countries)

The economist's assessment that the BRICS era is at an end is right on the money. Despite witnessing robust economic growth in the last decade, each of the BRICS countries faces a unique set of problems today. The recent global economic downturn has exposed structural infirmities that will prevent these economies from returning to a high growth trajectory any-
5   time soon. Besides, neither is it realistic to expect these emerging markets to grow faster from a higher GDP base than their previous low threshold.

In India, the economy is wracked by a rupee in free fall (by over 30%), high inflation (touching double digits), and a burgeoning current account deficit (almost 5% of GDP). Recent months
10   have seen significant capital outflows with foreign investors opting to park their funds in a recovering US economy. The petering out of growth sentiments is directly related to the fail-ure of the political leadership to affect a much-needed second wave of economic reforms. And with policy paralysis expected to be sustained, the India growth story remains in limbo. In both Brazil and Russia, the weakening of commodity prices has hit the economies hard, exposing
15   their over-reliance on natural resources as cash cows. Meanwhile, South Africa's economy has been hurting since a recession that affected several crucial industries. In China, the economy is transitioning from resource-intensive, investment-led growth to a consumption-oriented pat-tern. Add to this the massive global pressure to appreciate the yuan, and it is clear that China

would need to affect a not-so-easy overhaul of its economic model to maintain high growth.
20 However, as the economist points out, given China's planned economic model and ability to move resources without political missteps, it is best placed among the BRICS nations to pull out of the middle-income trap. Taken together, the global heft that the BRICS bloc wielded is over. And while these emerging markets will continue to grow, they will need to get used to moderate rates of growth.

Question 1

On which of the following aspects will the authors of both passages agree?

(A)   Acknowledging that BRICS countries experienced good economic growth in the past

(B)   The timeframe in which BRICS countries will bounce back to good economic growth

(C)   The ability of China to transform into a consumption-oriented economy soon

(D)   The growth prospects of the Indian economy

Question 2

Which of the following CANNOT be inferred based on the information provided?

(A)   Brazil and Russia's economies are dependent on natural resources.

(B)   The US economy is benefitting in some way due to current economic problems occurring in one of the BRICS countries.

(C)   The weakening of commodity prices in Brazil and Russia benefitted China.

(D)   Russia, Brazil, and South Africa each account for much less than 40% of Greenfield FDI projects in BRICS.

Question 3

Which of the following rhetorical devices has been used by both passages?

(A)   personal observation

(B)   hypothetical situations

(C)   quantitative information

(D)   comparison of groups

Question 4

Unlike the author of Passage 1, the author of Passage 2 believes that China

(A)   will not march far ahead of the other BRICS nations

(B)   will perform the best among the BRICS nations

(C)   will be overtaken by India in the near future

(D)   does not attract Greenfield investments

Question 5

Which of the following provides the best evidence for the belief of the author of passage 2 that China will perform the best among the BRICS nations?

(A)   Lines 8-9 (In India, the . . . 5% of GDP)

(B)   Lines 21-23 (However, as the . . . middle-income trap)

(C)   Lines 17-18 (In China, the . . . oriented pattern)

(D)   Lines 24-25 (And while . . . of growth)

Question 6

Which contrast best describes how the author of each passage views the future prospects of the BRICS nations?

(A)   The author of Passage 1 believes that all BRICS nations will march ahead, while the author of Passage 2 believes that none will.

(B)   The author of Passage 1 suggests that only India will grow, but the author of Passage 2 feels that India will languish.

(C)   The author of Passage 1 suggests that BRICS nations will continue to grow, whereas the author of Passage 2 feels that only China can progress.

(D)   The author of Passage 1 feels China will be overtaken by other BRICS nations, while the author of Passage 2 feels that China will supersede every other nation.

Question 7

The author of Passage 2 has a positive and negative opinion about the growth prospects of which of the following pairs of countries in the correct, respective order?

(A)   China and South Africa

(B)   India and China

(C)   India and Brazil

(D)   China and US

Question 8

With which of the following options will both the authors agree about India?

(A)   India's growth prospects are dismal.

(B)   India has had to bear capital flow reversals.

(C)   India's economy is strong enough to turn around.

(D)   India needs a round of economic reforms.

Question 9

In the two passages, the highlighted phrase "peter out" most nearly means

(A) vanish

(B) mushroom

(C) abate

(D) exacerbate

The following two questions are based on the following graph.

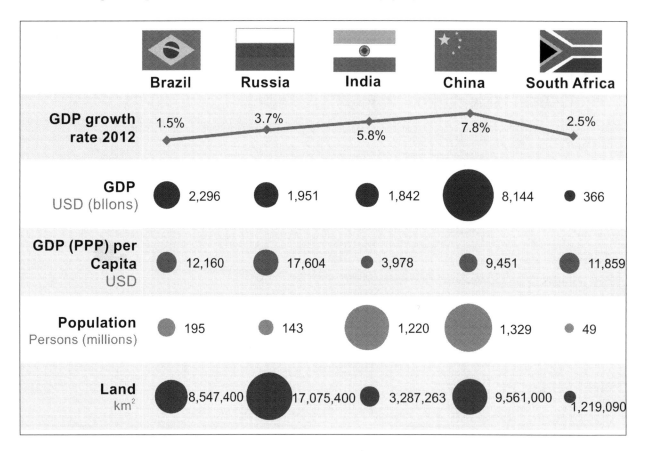

Question 10

Which of the following deductions is supported by the graph?

(A) Among the BRICS countries, the country that has the highest GDP also has the largest population and the highest GDP per Capita income.

(B) Among the BRICS countries, the country that has the largest land does not have the largest or the highest value for any of the remaining four parameters.

(C) Among the BRICS countries, the country that has the lowest population does not have the largest or the highest value for any of the remaining four parameters.

(D) Among the BRICS countries, the country that has the highest GDP growth rate also has the largest or the highest values for at least three parameters of the remaining parameters.

Question 11

Among the four counties – Brazil, Russia, India, and China – which had the highest land to population ratio (Sq. km/million)?

(A) Brazil

(B) Russia

(C) India

(D) China

5.11   Passage 11: Paired passage (Biographies on Hemingway)

Passage 1 (Dillon-Malone's biography on Hemingway)

Nowhere in his derivative biography does Aubrey Dillon-Malone explain why he felt the world needed another Hemingway biography. A Dublin-based novelist, Dillon-Malone seems to have stumbled upon his subject in the same way that Michael Palin did: through a fascination with Hemingway's singular form of American celebrity. Indeed, the recurring focus on Hemingway's
5   "Americanness" is the only element of this work that distinguishes it from Kurt Singer's and Milt Machlin's biographies. Those works were dubbed by Philip Young as "vulture biographies," and Dillon-Malone's biography, like those by Singer and Machlin, feeds without attribution from earlier, careful work by serious Hemingway biographers. By sloppily blending the all too familiar facts of Hemingway's life with the equally familiar echoes in his fiction, Dillon-Malone
10   has generated 358 pages of prose that only occasionally generate glimmers of interest for the reader. Dillon-Malone's goal is to lay down the "facts" of Hemingway's life to pierce the bubble of the "Hemingway legend." Many sentences are organized around phrases such as "the truth of the incident" or "the reality of the situation." This absence of nuance may engage read-ers who are tired of scanning footnotes and deciphering carefully reasoned opinions, yet the
15   unearned authoritative biographical voice of Dillon-Malone is difficult to trust even on simple matters. Paradoxically, Dillon-Malone celebrates the same values he critiques. As Hemingway scholarship has moved far beyond the confines of this "legendary image," Dillon-Malone's in-terpretation is not especially refreshing or enlightening.Perhaps the only thing to be learned from this biography is Dillon-Malone's opinion of Hemingway. His impressions are decisive,
20   judgmental, and predictable. According to Dillon-Malone, Hemingway was an uneven writer, and a disappointment as a human being. There is very little thoughtful commentary here on Hemingway's fiction. In sum, even as a celebrity biography aiming to entertain a mass-market audience, *Hemingway: The Grace and the Pressure* misses its mark. Derivative, repetitive, and poorly organized, the book manages to make a dramatic life dull. Divorces, plane crashes, fist-
25   fights, and war wounds are recounted in a style that is crude and heavy-handed. Dillon-Malone has done no original research, and all of the twenty-four black and white photos are overly familiar. Dillon-Malone's biography only deserves a place on the lowest bookshelf beside the works of Milt Machlin, Kurt Singer, and Peter Buckley.

Passage 2 (Wagner-Martin's biography on Hemingway)

Unlike his contemporaries Fitzgerald and Steinbeck, Ernest Hemingway managed to maintain a literary dominance that continued steadily during his life and has wavered only slightly in the years since his death in 1961. Linda Wagner-Martin's "*Earnest Hemingway*" constitutes an indispensable source for general readers and scholars alike as we enter the new century. As
5   Wagner-Martin notes in her introduction, Hemingway–although an "incurable romantic"–was remarkable for the serious way in which he addressed the business of writing. In addition to his unique, economic style, and his portraits of life that shocked and intrigued many of his early readers, he influenced the entire genre of "hard-boiled" mystery and detective fiction. Through his writing as well as his public persona, his pursuit and successful achievement of
10   the American dream positions him as an engaging subject for a historically-focused examina-tion, for Hemingway metaphorically represents and reflects the issues that preoccupied Amer-icans of his era: issues of world war, of gender, of industry and ecology, and of human triumph and loss. One theoretical method that has recently benefited Hemingway scholarship is inter-

15 textuality, the borrowing of or references to other fictional works. Wagner-Martin identifies numerous ways in which Hemingway responds to the fiction and the writers of his time. Indeed, so deeply was Hemingway immersed in literature of both the 19th and the 20th centuries that, in adapting those works to his own art, he became a pioneer in the technique of inter-textuality. Citing a number of writers and novels that influenced Hemingway, Wagner-Martin

20 discusses in particular Hemingway's extensive use of Henry James, and she draws several significant conclusions about the ways in which Hemingway wanted readers to see that he was different from–and, he doubtless hoped, better than–these older masters. After all, he actually told Charles Scribner that he wanted to "beat dead writers" that he considered first-rate artists.

25 This superb handbook for understanding Hemingway in our own time is followed by an extremely useful illustrated chronology that parallels events in Hemingway's own life with concurrent historical events and publication dates of other significant literature. Wagner-Martin's book is an invaluable tool for both the general reader and the Hemingway scholar: indeed, ignoring this book would render much of Hemingway disappointingly inaccessible to the contemporary reader.

Question 1

Both the authors are primarily discussing

(A) Hemingway's life

(B) works of Hemingway

(C) works on Hemingway

(D) Hemingway's persona

Question 2

Unlike Passage 2, Passage 1 employs the following rhetorical device.

(A) comparisons with other similar works

(B) attributions from important sources

(C) detailed critique of the work in discussion

(D) personal opinions about the work in discussion

Question 3

Which of the following could be inferred as the opinion, on Hemingway, of the author of Passage 1?

(A) He led a colorful life.

(B) He was an uneven writer.

(C) He had a dull life.

(D) He is disappointing as a human being.

Question 4

Which book would be important for a person trying to understand Hemingway's works, as can be gathered from the information in the two passages?

(A)   Hemingway: the Grace and the Pressure

(B)   Earnest Hemingway

(C)   the biography by Peter Buckley

(D)   the biography by Michael Palin

Question 5

Unlike Passage 1, Passage 2 makes

(A)   contrasts with other biographies

(B)   attributions from important sources

(C)   a detailed evaluation of the biography

(D)   personal opinions about the biography

Question 6

According to the author of Passage 1, Dillon-Malone wrote a biography on Hemingway because of

(A)   his fascination with Hemingway's peculiar fame

(B)   Hemingway's facts and fiction

(C)   his admiration for Hemingway's writing

(D)   a lack of good biography on Hemingway

Question 7

According to the author of Passage 2, Wagner-Martin's book is important because

(A)   there are not enough biographies on Hemingway

(B)   it provides present-day readers with the requisite perspective

(C)   intertextuality has not been discussed by any other work at all

(D)   Ernest Hemingway has continued to fascinate old and new readers alike

Question 8

Which of the following best describes the relationship between the first and the second passages, in their verdict of the biographies they critique?

(A) The author of Passage 1 endorses the work, as does the author of Passage 2.

(B) The author of Passage 1 cautiously appreciates the work, whereas the author of Passage 2 wholeheartedly approves of it.

(C) The author of Passage 1 criticizes the work, and the author of Passage 2 remains neutral about it.

(D) The author of Passage 1 disparages the work, while the author of Passage 2 finds the work exceptional.

Question 9

Which of the following lines provides evidence to explain why Hemingway was so persistently famous among all?

(A) Passage 2: Lines 1-3 (Unlike his contemporaries . . . death in 1961)

(B) Passage 2: Lines 3-5 (Linda Wagner-Martin's . . . we enter the new century)

(C) Passage 2: Lines 9-14 (Through his writing . . . triumph and loss)

(D) Passage 1: Lines 2-4 (A Dublin-based . . . American celebrity)

Question 10

Which of the following can be inferred as Hemingway's beliefs from the information given in the passages above?

(A) Hemingway considered Henry James an accomplished writer.

(B) Hemingway was conscious of his fame and position as an American icon.

(C) Hemingway wished to beat Fitzgerald and Steinbeck in literary dominance.

(D) Hemingway wished to identify with the general public by reflecting on world war.

Chapter 6

Answer Key

Passage 1

(1) C	(4) A	(7) C	(10) D
(2) C	(5) A	(8) B	
(3) D	(6) B	(9) A	(11) C

Passage 2

(1) D	(4) B	(7) C	(10) A
(2) D	(5) D	(8) B	
(3) A	(6) A	(9) B	(11) C

Passage 3

(1) B	(4) B	(7) B	(10) C
(2) B	(5) A	(8) A	
(3) C	(6) B	(9) A	(11) D

Passage 4

(1) A	(4) C	(7) D	(10) A
(2) C	(5) A	(8) B	
(3) C	(6) C	(9) A	(11) A

Passage 5

(1) D	(4) C	(7) B	(10) C
(2) D	(5) C	(8) D	
(3) C	(6) D	(9) C	(11) B

Passage 6

(1) A	(4) A	(7) D	(10) C
(2) A	(5) C	(8) D	
(3) C	(6) B	(9) B	(11) B

Passage 7

(1) C	(4) B	(7) C	(10) B
(2) B	(5) A	(8) C	
(3) C	(6) D	(9) D	(11) C

Passage 8

(1) A	(4) D	(7) D	(10) B
(2) B	(5) A	(8) C	
(3) A	(6) C	(9) B	(11) A

Passage 9

(1) D	(4) D	(7) A	(10) D
(2) D	(5) A	(8) A	
(3) B	(6) C	(9) C	(11) B

Passage 10

(1) A	(4) B	(7) A	(10) C
(2) C	(5) B	(8) B	
(3) C	(6) C	(9) C	(11) B

Passage 11

(1) C	(4) B	(7) B	(10) A
(2) A	(5) B	(8) D	
(3) A	(6) A	(9) C	

Chapter 7

Solutions

7.1 Passage 1 (Climate change due to volcanic eruptions)

Understanding the Passage

This is a long passage of high difficulty level. You should spend 5-6 minutes to read the passage and 60-75 seconds to answer each question; so, in all, you should spend approximately 14-15 minutes on a passage.

Iceland is one of the most volcanic places on the planet, with over 160 volcanoes; and it experiences a major volcanic eruption almost every decade. The close proximity to Europe and the prevailing western winds make it possible for volcanic ash and gases to reach the continent. *(Iceland is one of the most volcanic places. It is close to Europe and has a system of Western winds. All this combined makes ash and gases reach the rest of Europe.)* One of the most notable and best documented events was the eruption of the Laki Volcano in 1873. The eruption started on 8 June and lasted for eight months, producing 15 cubic kilometers of lava.

There have been many previous studies that have focused on understanding the potential role of Icelandic volcanic eruptions in modifying the environment; they have concentrated on the degree of induced climate change; however, the complex interaction of the processes which control the atmospheric circulation patterns of the earth were imperfectly understood when such studies were being conducted, and even with advanced equipment have proved difficult to model. Thus, studies have not taken into account these complex interactions when looking at the role of Icelandic volcanic eruptions in affecting the environment and bringing about climate change. *(There were previous studies which checked whether Icelandic volcanic eruptions have the potential to modify the environment. These studies concentrated on the degree of "induced" or brought-about climate change [as opposed to natural climate change]. However, even then, the complexities of the interaction processes that control the atmosphere were not fully understood. Even with advanced equipment, they were difficult to model into accurate conceptual details. The inference the author wants to drive is that those studies would be, at best, limited, given the lack of understanding of the processes.)*

One of the main ideas put forth is that in 1783, volcanic gases emitted by the eruption in Iceland were transported to Europe by the prevailing winds, where they caused considerable respiratory distress to susceptible people, and damage to crops, trees, and fish. Documentary

103

evidence suggests that during the Laki fissure eruption, severe acid damage to crops occurred in northern Europe and acid pulses killed fish in Scotland as the discharge of sulfuric and hydrofluoric acid continued over many weeks after the initial eruptions. *(There is evidence that a volcanic eruption in Laki [Iceland], in 1783, released acid that probably caused crop damage and killed fish in Northern Europe, possibly modifying the environment.)* These studies also propose that upper troposphere and lower stratosphere aerosols from Laki disrupted the thermal balance of the Arctic regions for two summers and were the main mechanism for the associated climate **perturbations**. *(These studies state that Laki's discharge in the upper troposphere and lower stratosphere affected the Arctic region for two summers and is mainly responsible for climate change.)* Although an induced climatic change that was the result of the volcanic eruption was probably the primary mechanism responsible for the main damage to crops and ecology in the surrounding area, the degree to which atmospheric circulation of winds responds to volcanic eruption and forcing is uncertain, so it is unsatisfactory to suggest that stress in the paleo-environmental record, associated with a volcanic eruption, has inevitably occurred in response to volcanic forcing of climate. *(While we can say that it was not natural climate change, but an induced one that caused the damage, the degree to which the Laki volcano forced the change cannot be determined. So, we must not suggest that volcanic eruption forced the climate change and brought about paleo-environmental* (an environment in the geological past) *stress (power) [killing fish and damaging crops] was directly a result of that eruption).* The only volcanic eruptions which possess the theoretical ability to bring about climate change are those which emit substantial volumes of volatile gases. "Climate change theories" require that these gases be injected into the stratosphere and remain in the troposphere. *(Theories state that these emitted gases from such volcanic eruptions are injected into the stratosphere* (the lowest densest part of the earth's atmosphere in which most weather changes occur) *and remain in the troposphere* (the second major layer of Earth's atmosphere, just above the troposphere)). They must inevitably settle and be deposited on the surrounding sea and land rather than distant ecosystems. Despite plenty of excavations, such sedimentary evidence still eludes researchers around the Laki central fissure. *(These gases will typically settle and be deposited on the surrounding sea of the volcanic eruptions and not in some distant land).* Despite plenty of excavations, such sedimentary evidence still eludes researchers around the Laki central fissure. *(No sedimentation, the kind associated with the climate-changing volcanic eruptions, has been found around the Laki area. The inference being implied here is that it is unlikely Laki brought about the kind of climate change that is believed.)*

Admittedly, many crops withered because of the acid deposition, but there are no reports on the continent of famine. This was different in northern Scotland ,where the population was facing hardship because of a harvest failure in 1782, a year before the eruption. *(While crops were damaged, famine was not caused by the eruption. Famine happened in Scotland because it already had harvest failure before the eruption.)* The food situation was already poor when acid deposition and ash from the Laki eruption rained down and destroyed crops. *(The volcanic eruption only worsened a bad situation.)* Reports from northern Scotland suggest that many farmers and their families abandoned their farms and 'were forced to beg or perish. This shows that the effects of the Laki eruption were not the direct cause of famine in Northern Scotland, but the last straw which triggered the crisis. *(Thus, the volcano did not cause any famine, but worsened a bad situation.)*

Thus, perhaps the 1873 Laki eruption contributed to more serious consequences for the Icelandic population. Iceland depended heavily on sheep and cattle herding as a source of food production, along with some production of grain and other crops. Acid deposition stunted the growth of grass, affecting fodder production to feed animals during the winter months. In addition, fluorine deposition poisoned streams and grass, killing around 80 percent of sheep and half of all cattle. As a result, an estimated 20-25 percent of the population died in the famine and fluorine poisoning after the fissure eruptions ceased. Volcanic eruptions are inadequate to explain social and ecological changes. Climatic and environmental disasters are, most of the time, "funnels", and not direct causes of long term historical developments. They reinforce already existing historical patterns, such as migration or political instability, over exploitation or the development of new economic and social regimes. *(The volcanic eruption more seriously affected the Icelandic population, but not the rest of Europe. It may have worsened some existing situations in Europe, but did not drive climate change or any other change. Thus, the author is negating the studies and the theories mentioned earlier.)*

In the above passage, the author starts by introducing the concept that volcanic eruptions are thought to cause induced climate change but immediately presents the fact that there's not enough evidence to say so because the degree of complex atmospheric interactions isn't understood yet. He further makes this point using the Laki eruption, which is believed to have caused damage in Northern Europe, and possibly brought about climate change. However, the author explains that if the Laki eruption had brought about climate change, there would be volcanic emissions that would have settled around the sea and land. Such deposits haven't been found yet, so it is likely that the Laki eruption did not cause, not fully, the climate change.

Main Point: To prove that volcanic eruptions are not very likely to cause induced climate change, and not to the degree believed.

Question 1-Solution

This is a main purpose question from the general category.

In the above passage, the author starts by introducing the concept that volcanic eruptions are thought to cause induced climate change but immediately presents the fact that there's not enough evidence to say so because the degree of complex atmospheric interactions isn't understood yet. He further makes this point using the Laki eruption, which is believed to have caused damage in Northern Europe, and possibly brought about climate change. However, the author explains that if the Laki eruption had brought about climate change, there would be volcanic emissions that would have settled around the sea and land. Such deposits haven't been found yet, so it is likely that the Laki eruption did not cause, not fully, the climate change. Also, the author states that the situation in Scotland and the rest of Europe was worsened, but not caused by, the volcanic eruption.

Thus, his main point is to prove that volcanic eruptions are not very likely to cause induced climate change, and not to the degree believed. The author wishes to negate the studies that suggest that the volcano induced climate change.

Let's analyze the options one by one.

(A)   This option is **incorrect** because the author does not discuss various theories as the main purpose. He merely presents them to make one point only. This is not his main purpose.

(B) This option is **incorrect** because the author does not provide any evidence towards explaining climate change in Northern Europe, but merely explains that there is lack of such.

(C) This is the **correct** answer. This matches our deductions.

(D) This option is **incorrect** because the author does not discuss any controversial hypothesis at all.

The correct answer is C.

Question 2-Solution

This is a detail question.

The question asks us to locate some detail about the previous studies of volcanic eruptions. This is mentioned in the first paragraph. There were previous studies to check whether Icelandic volcanic eruptions have the potential to modify the environment. However, the complexities of the interaction processes that control the atmosphere were not fully understood. Even with advanced equipment, they were difficult to model into accurate conceptual details.

Let's analyze the options one by one.

(A) This option is **incorrect** because the passage states that the eruptions were likely not responsible for the climate change.

(B) This option is **incorrect** because the previous studies were more likely accepted by existing theories than not. We cannot necessarily say that they were rejected.

(C) This is the **correct** answer. This matches our deductions.

(D) This option is **incorrect** because the passage states that the eruptions were likely not responsible for the climate change.

The correct answer is C.

Question 3 -Solution

This is a specific inference question.

We know that there is evidence that a volcanic eruption in Laki in 1783 released acid that probably caused crop damage and killed fish in Northern Europe, possibly modifying the environment. However, the degree to which the Laki volcano forced the change cannot be determined. So, we must not suggest that volcanic eruption forced the climate change and brought about paleo-environmental stress [killing fish and damaging crops] as a result of that eruption. Also, no sedimentation has been found around the Laki area and thus there is no proof that Laki brought about the kind of climate change as is believed.

Let's analyze the options one by one.

(A) This option is **incorrect** because no such thing is mentioned in the passage.

(B) This option is **incorrect** because no such evidence is presented in the passage to infer this.

(C) This option is **incorrect** because this is the opposite of the implied inference. The author makes a case to suggest that the degree to which eruption could affect the change in the climate of Northern Europe is uncertain. The evidence in Laki also does not support it; hence, we cannot say that the eruptions did so.

(D) This is the **correct** answer. This matches our deductions.

The correct answer is D.

Question 4-Solution

This is a reasoning question on weakening the conclusion.

The question asks us to prove the author incorrect and prove that Icelandic eruptions did bring about induced climate change. We need to find evidence to prove that. The author bases his claim that the Icelandic eruption probably did **not** bring about induced climate change on the lack of sedimentation associated with the climate-changing volcanic eruptions around the Laki area. Thus, to prove that Icelandic eruptions did bring about induced climate change, we need to prove either that the Laki volcano emitted volatile gases that were injected into the stratosphere and troposphere and that eventually got deposited in the surrounding land and sea. Such evidence would prove the author incorrect.

Let's analyze the options one by one.

(A) This is the **correct** answer. This matches our deductions.

(B) This option is **incorrect** because the author does not deny that the Laki eruptions caused environmental stress, but he disputes that such stress brought about induced climate change. Hence, this would not prove the author wrong.

(C) This option is **incorrect** because this would not prove the author wrong. He does not dispute that fish and crops were affected. He disputes their link with climate change brought about by volcanic eruptions.

(D) This option is **incorrect** because this is out of scope. Mere climate fluctuations do not necessarily prove the author wrong that volcanic eruption causing those fluctuations led to climate change. Climatic fluctuation is a temporary phenomenon, and climate change is permanent.

The correct answer is A.

Question 5 -Solution

This is a function question from the general category.

We are asked to find the purpose of the second paragraph with respect to the third and fourth paragraphs, i.e. why the second paragraph is explaining what it is, and how that relates to the third and fourth paragraphs' point of view. The third and fourth paragraphs prove the point that the Icelandic eruption probably did **not** bring about induced climate change. The second paragraph discusses the belief that the Icelandic eruptions did bring about induced climate change, only to later say that there's not enough evidence to say so because the degree of complex atmospheric interactions isn't understood yet. Thus, the author makes a point in the second paragraph and then explains it in detail in the third and fourth paragraphs. So, the second paragraph served as a sort of introduction to the details in the third and fourth paragraphs.

Let's analyze the options one by one.

(A) This is the **correct** answer. This matches our deductions.

(B) This option is **incorrect** because the author makes the opposite point, that the climate change was not the result of volcanic eruption completely.

(C) This option is **incorrect** because this point is being made in the second paragraph. The first paragraph merely states this point but the second paragraph **proves** it. This is a tricky option.

(D) This option is **incorrect** because the author implies the opposite of this in the entire passage.

The correct answer is A.

Question 6 -Solution

This is an inference question.

We have been asked to infer the meaning of the highlighted word "perturbations" as used in the passage in the third paragraph. Let's analyze the sentence in which this word is used: *"... aerosols from Laki **disrupted** the thermal balance of the Arctic regions ... and were the main mechanism for the **associated** climate perturbations. Although an **induced climatic change** that was ..."* Thus, volcano disrupted balance and "perturbations" were an associated effect. Also, later on this entire thing is referred to as *"induced climate change"*. Thus, "perturbations" must mean "change/disruption".

Let's analyze the options one by one.

(A) This option is **incorrect** because "activity" only means some action but not necessarily "change". It is too generic and dilute.

(B) This option is **correct** because "turmoil" means "change and disruption". This matches our deductions.

(C) This option is **incorrect** because "repression" means "subdue or curb or control" but there is no context for control or subdue in the sentence.

(D) This option is **incorrect** because "domination" also means to "control" and has a negative hint to it. However, we cannot necessarily state that "perturbations" is either negative or involves "control".

The correct answer is B.

Question 7 -Solution

We have been asked to select a sentence from the final paragraph that **substantiates** (provides proof) the statement that the Laki volcano eruption affected the Icelandic population.

Let's analyze the options one by one.

(A)   This option is **incorrect** because this sentence merely presents the statement we're supposed to prove, but does not provide any substantiation or proof.

(B)   This option is **incorrect** because this statement only shows dependency of the Icelandic population on certain things, but not how the volcano affected the population.

(C)   This option is **correct** because this statement provides proof that the Laki volcano eruption affected the Icelandic population by killing cattle.

(D)   This option is **incorrect** because this is a generic statement not providing any proof.

The correct answer is C.

Question 8 -Solution

This is an inference question.

We have been asked to present the author's opinion about the connection between the Laki volcano and the situation in Northern Scotland. The answer to this lies in the penultimate paragraph, in which the author states that the situation in Northern Scotland was bad even before the volcano erupted. The eruption did not cause the famine, but worsened the situation.

Let's analyze the options one by one.

(A)   This option is **incorrect** because the author believes that the explosion only worsened the existing situation in Scotland, but did not primarily cause it.

(B)   This option is **correct** because this is close to the author's belief. This matches our deductions above.

(C)   This option is **incorrect** because the author states, in the final paragraph, that eruptions don't bring about ecological or social changes.

(D)   This option is **incorrect** because this is contradictory to the author's statement.

The correct option is B.

Question 9 -Solution

This is a function question from the general category.

We have been asked to find the purpose of the first line of the fourth paragraph: *Admittedly, many crops withered because of the acid deposition, but there are no reports on the continent of famine.* The author states that the eruption damaged crops, but did not cause famine. The author then explains that famine happened in Northern Scotland only because the situation there was already bad. The author eventually concludes that effects of the Laki eruption were not the direct cause of famine in Northern Scotland, but were the last straw which triggered the crisis. Thus, his first line is to suggest that the volcano cannot be blamed for any famine, in Europe or in Scotland.

Let's analyze the options one by one.

(A)   This option is **correct** because this matches our deductions above.

(B)   This option is **incorrect** because while the sentence contains discussions of the effects of the eruption, this is not the purpose of the sentence. The sentence is intended to prove that the volcano did not cause famine.

(C)   This option is **incorrect** because the author does not suggest this about famine in general; the author believes that in Northern Scotland the eruption only worsened, but did not cause, the famine.

(D)   This option is **incorrect** because even though the sentence contains discussions of the effects of the eruption, this is not the purpose of the sentence. The sentence is intended to prove that the volcano did not cause famine.

The correct answer is A.

Chart for questions # 10 & 11

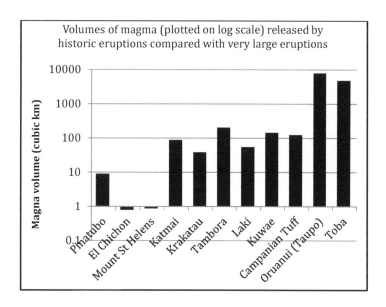

Question 10 -Solution

The median of a series of data is given by the middle-most value if the data in the series are arranged in ascending or in descending order.

Though it is difficult to read the data, it is not required to have the values, as the question asks for the name of the volcanic eruptions, representing median magna volume and not its numerical value of median magna volume.

Let us choose to arrange the 11 volcanic eruptions in ascending order of their magna volumes. The middle-most value would be the 6th one ($\frac{11+1}{2} = 6$).

If we arrange the values in ascending order, we observe that three smaller values belong to El Chichon, Mount St Helens, and Pinatubo. Though we cannot be sure of the 4th and 5th ones, it is not needed; they would be Krakatau and Laki. And the 6th one is Katmai, the required answer.

The correct answer is option D.

Question 11 -Solution

Like the previous question, though the question requires values, they are not needed, as the options are the names of the volcanic eruptions and not their values.

We can get the differences in magna volumes by visual inspection.

Option A can certainly be in the reckoning, the difference in magna volumes of Toba & Oruanui seems to be less. However, option B cannot be the answer, as this could, in fact, be the answer for the largest difference between any pair of magna volumes. The magna volumes of Kuwae & Campanian Tuff are too close and their values look almost equal, hence option C could be the answer. The difference in the magna volumes of Laki & Tambora is relatively more than that of Kuwae & Campanian Tuff, hence it is ruled out; additionally, the difference between the values for Toba and Oruanui is more than the difference between the values for Kuwae and Campanian Tuff; thus C is the answer.

The correct answer is option C.

7.2 Passage 2 (In-fighting Indian princes and the rise of the British)

Understanding the Passage

This is a long passage of low difficulty level on history.

For 17th century Europeans, the history of Eastern empires was stereotyped. India's historical events were predictable customs of unrefined and stereotypical traditional stories. According to the traditional story, typically, the founder of an empire would be a brave soldier and a frantic conspirator who would topple corrupt scions of a more ancient empire. The founder's son may inherit some of his talent; but in two or three generations, descendants become immoral and corrupt and are dethroned by some new adventurer. *[Thus, in the British's mind, whenever anyone is dethroned in Eastern empires, it is justified because according to them the person sitting on the throne is a descendent of a brave person, but does not have the appropriate qualities to rule correctly and should be overthrown/removed from the throne.]* Thus an upright rebellion will dethrone a corrupt empire and subsequently be dethroned by another rebellion. *[This is how they rationalize creating and orchestrating rebellions to remove the existing rulers.]* This practice was on-going. This led to recurrence of civil war and anarchy at fixed intervals. Due to these anarchistic practices, Britain's rulers could visualize their might in the subcontinent. *[Using such tactics, the British were virtually in control because they removed the rulers who could potentially disagree with the British and put in such rulers who would end up being puppets in the British's hands, thereby ensuring British interests.]* The British wished to avoid the bloodshed periodically occurring during the toppling of an empire and this led them to gain the favor of India's local empires. *[They played a diplomatic game by removing the current ruler and backing a new ruler, and they thus avoided actual wars but gained favors from the newly installed ruler.]*

British armies and British administrators were able to insinuate rule over India by two primary methods. *[The British used two primary methods to insinuate (maneuver into place with cunning) themselves into power over India]* The first of these was the outright annexation of Indian states and subsequent direct governance of the underlying regions. *[At times, they just directly used power to grab the states and took over direct ruling of such states and their regions.]* The second form of asserting power involved treaties in which Indian rulers acknowledged the Company's hegemony in return for limited internal autonomy. *[The second form was a bit indirect. They dominated rulers by signing treaties in which the rulers gave recognition to the British authority in the state.]* Since the Company operated under financial constraints, it had to set up political underpinnings for its rule. *[The Company wanted to set up its rule but with limited financial involvement.]* The most important such support came from the subsidiary alliances with Indian princes during the first 75 years of Company rule. *[To set themselves up, the British got into subsidiary alliances by which they practically established their dominion with very little financial input.]* The British were able to impose a proxy rule over India by setting up native princes in positions of power. It is to be noted that Indian empires used to follow the law of "doctrines of lapse", which means that if the ruling king dies without any sons *(heirs)*, any of the related princes *(nephews)* can lay claim to the empire. British used to support any one of the princes, and to maintain his power as long as it was in their interests. *[If there are two possible candidates for the throne, they would support the one who would further their interests the most and put him on the throne.]* In this way the princes became practically obliged to cooperate with the British. And the result was two generations of trivial tyrant princes, protected by the British. These tyrant princes spent their lives in apathetic dishonesty, cruelty, and oppression. *[The rulers chosen by the British were always bad ones but could not be removed because they were protected by British might.]*

The passage is about how the British could enforce their rule over India, their strategy, and tactics. The British took advantage of in-fighting among princes to claim the empire once the leadership of it lapsed. The British used to support a prince and make him the king, and, by doing this, the new king would be obliged to the British. Unfortunately the king under the shadow of the British would become corrupt and cruel.

Main Point: In-fighting among the princes of the Indian Empire and tactics by the British to impose a proxy rule in India.

Question 1-Solution

This is an inference question.

Option D is the best answer because the passage speaks of the British in the following way: "Their methods took advantage of existing "doctrines of lapse", and made use of what was already the declared law in cases of heredity. By intervening on behalf of one prince or another, both of whom may have been equally suited to claim the right to the throne in cases in which the rights to leadership lapsed, they put themselves in a position to support a leader they selected, and to maintain his power as long as it was in their interests. In this way the princes became practically obliged to cooperate with the British.". So, they ruled by proxy *(indirectly)* by making the ruler obliged to them. Thus, their proxy rule can be attributed to the "doctrine of lapse".

Other options are not discussed in the passage and so cannot be necessarily inferred.

The correct answer is D.

Question 2-Solution

This is an inference question.

(A)   This option is **incorrect** because we cannot compare the situations prevailing before and after the British came to India. It is out of scope of the passage.

(B)   This option is **incorrect** because the reverse of this option is true. On the contrary, the author may disagree that British intervention in India was a positive influence on India. The scheming done by the British sustained their favorite, yet corrupt and incapable, kings as the monarchs who otherwise would have been dethroned by brave, upright rebellions.

(C)   This option is **incorrect** because it is too extreme and cannot be inferred from the passage.

(D)   This is the **correct** answer. The passage suggests that had the British not intervened, the cycle of change of power would have taken place at a fixed interval, and at least periodically, India would have a competent king followed by corrupt kings. But because of the

British's supporting of their favorite, yet corrupt and incapable, kings as the monarch did not make way for change of leadership. Thus, British interference led to a necessarily bad king, whereas without the British, India would have had good kings sooner or later.

The correct answer is D.

Question 3 -Solution

This is a tone question from the general category.

(A)   This is the **correct** answer because the author laments the constant decline of kings into "feeble inheritors"; he notes that feeble inheritors fostered by the British have done more bad than good for India.

(B)   This option is **incorrect** because the author endorses that a change of power by a rebellion is the remedy to get rid of cruel kings. He does not despair of it or give it up.

(C)   This option is **incorrect** because the author is not skeptical of the prevailing cycle of rule. He rather acknowledges it.

(D)   This option is **incorrect** because we can't say that he necessarily approves of the cycle of rule. He acknowledges it as something that has worked out fairly well, but that does not mean he likes it and approves of it. He may believe that there might be a better way. All we can say is that he certainly disapproves of the British's interference and that he accepts that the cycle of rule works better when left alone, but we can't say that he approves of it necessarily.

The correct answer is A.

Question 4-Solution

This is an inference question.

(A)   This option is **incorrect** because according to the passage, the people were not supposed to choose their leader; it's the hereditary cycle of rule that choose the leader.

(B)   This is the **correct** answer because the last two sentences of the passage endorse this: "The result was two generations of petty despots, insulated from the consequences of misrule by British bayonets. The despots spent their lives in listless debauchery, broken by paroxysms of cruelty and oppression". The British safeguarded their favorite, yet cruel, kings and did not let rebellions oust them, causing damage to the subcontinent. Thus, the rule continued because the Indian people did not have the sort of power needed to overcome British might.

(C)   This option is **incorrect** because the passage did not talk about the demoralization of the Indian identity.

(D)   This option is **incorrect** because while this is the reason the despot rulers were put on the throne, it is not necessarily damaging. The British can exploit the doctrine of lapse and put a prince on the throne, but this does not have to be damaging if they had put a good ruler there. However, the British were greedy to have indirect rule over India, so they always chose the leaders with low morality. Thus, we can attribute the damage to the British's attitude towards India or their greed, but not necessarily to the way they put people in power.

The correct answer is B.

Question 5 -Solution

This is an inference question.

Choice D is the best option, as it is exemplified by the British policy of coordinating with princes in need of support because British interest was to rule the Indian subcontinent by proxy and without bloodshed. Thus they cooperated when it was in their best interests to do so.

Other options are either not discussed in the passage or cannot necessarily be inferred.

The correct answer is D.

Question 6 -Solution

This is an inference question.

(A)   This is the **correct** answer because the British aided princes who were vulnerable and were competing with other princes. This action required little up front British influence in order to determine the outcome of the dispute, while making Britain the effective "kingmaker" in the region and allowing the British a great deal of influence later. This means that they had some amount of influence.

(B)   This option is **incorrect** because the British did not take over the leadership role themselves but put in rulers through whom they could rule by proxy.

(C)   This option is **incorrect** because the British were not helping the princes to discuss their dispute.

(D)   This option is **incorrect** because there were local candidates for leadership.

The correct answer is A.

Question 7 -Solution

This is a tone question from the general category.

Option C is the correct answer as is demonstrated by the British decision to seek to advance their own interests in India when it was possible to do so during times of disorder. Nothing else is possible to be attributed to the British in the given passage from among the options.

The correct answer is C.

Question 8 -Solution

This is a function question.

Let us understand the usage of the word *despotism*; it is used in the sentence: *Thus rebellion and deposition were the correctives of despotism, and therefore, a recurrence, at fixed intervals, of able and vigorous princes through the medium of periodical anarchy and civil war, occurred.*

The previous sentence to the above sentence—*His son may inherit some of the talent of the father, but in two or three generations, luxury and indolence do their work, and the feeble inheritors of a great name are dethroned by some new adventurer, destined to bequeath a like misfortune to his degenerate descendants.*—talks about the luxury and indolence (laziness, inactivity) of inheritors and rebellions were hailed for toppling these inheritors' autocratic rule, thus it can be inferred that despotism is used with reference to the oppressive rule of the inheritors, which also means tyranny, thus the correct answer is option B.

Though option A—stubborn (headstrong, willful), and option D—debauchery (depravity, immodesty) are negative by definition, they cannot be ideal replacements for despotism.

We cannot necessarily infer that the degenerate inheritors are stubborn or debauched.

The correct answer is B.

Question 9 -Solution

We have been asked to find a sentence containing evidence that the British used to justify their actions in India. This statement has to be from the first paragraph, which deals with the overview of the general behavior of the British and presents the reasons for their actions.

Let's analyze the options one by one.

(A) This option is **incorrect** because this sentence *"Thus rebellion and deposition were the correctives of despotism, and therefore, a recurrence, at fixed intervals, of able and vigorous princes through the medium of periodical anarchy and civil war, occurred"* is a general justification but not specific to the British. This is a general belief.

(B) This option is **correct** because this contains the justification that the British used for their actions in India. The sentence *"The rationale that justified their actions to the British public was that avoiding such upheaval to allow peaceful reign over India was their ultimate goal"* contains the reasons the British used to justify their actions to the British public, to suggest that by their intervention the period of constant fighting would stop and allow (their) peaceful reign.

(C) This option is **incorrect** because this statement *"According to similar typical accounts of Indian events, history unfolded itself with the predictable rituals of heavy-handed folklore"* is a typical belief that the Europeans have about Asia but is not necessarily specific to the British in India.

(D) This option is **incorrect** because this statement *"This founder's son may inherit some of the talent of the father; but in two or three generations luxury and indolence do their work, and the feeble inheritors of a great name are dethroned by some new adventurer, destined to bequeath a like misfortune to his degenerate descendants"* contains a detail about the general belief that the Europeans have about Asia.

The correct answer is B.

Question 10 -Solution

This is a reasoning question.

We have been asked to negate the ideas that Europeans have about Asians and Indians. Europeans, including the British, believed that Asia had a typical cycle in history, believed that a brave, rebellious founder dethrones a weak ruler, and that he may have sons but his dynasty becomes weak and then someone else dethrones his heirs. This is believed to go on and on, all because of a fixed, stereotyped perception (stated in line 11). To weaken these European ideas, their perception about Asian history needs to change, to become impartial, rather than stereotyped.

Let's analyze the options one by one.

(A)   This option is **correct** because this matches our deductions above.

(B)   This option is **incorrect** because this would be in keeping with their stereotyped beliefs.

(C)   This option is **incorrect** because this too may reinforce stereotypes of Europeans, since they believed that the sons of the rebellious, dynasty-creator could be talented but successive generations degenerated. This would not change European perceptions necessarily.

(D)   This option is **incorrect** because this would be in keeping with the European perceptions of constant cycles of bad rulers dethroned by rebellions.

The correct answer is A.

Question 11 -Solution

This is a main purpose question from the general category.

Titles should be given according to the main point of the passage. The passage is about how British could enforce their rule over India, their strategy, and tactic. The British took advantage of in-fighting among princes to claim for the empire once the leadership to it lapsed. The British used to support a prince and make him the kind and by doing this the new king would be obliged to the British. Unfortunately the king under the shadow of British would become corrupt and cruel.

Main Point: In-fighting among the princesses of Indian Empire and tactics by British to impose a proxy rule in India.

Let's analyze the options one by one.

(A)   This option is **incorrect** because while the sentence contains discussions of the British invasion, "British Life" would suggest discussions of their existence here. However, the passage merely discusses the various ways by which the British manipulated themselves into power.

(B) This option is **incorrect** because it is too general. The passage discusses greater details than mere European perceptions. The passage discusses Europeans in general, but British tactics in greater detail. The passage centers on the British and not on Europeans at large.

(C) This option is **correct** because this matches our deductions above.

(D) This option is **incorrect** because this option suggests the author feels that the British are the vigorous champions over tyrannical princes of India. However, the author implies that the British used various cunning ways to manipulate themselves into power and ended up putting corrupt and cruel rulers into place.

The correct answer is C.

7.3   Passage 3 (The Belgian economy: from devastation to restoration)

Understanding the Passage

This is a medium length passage of medium difficulty level on business policy and economics.

For 200 years until WW I, Wallonia, a part of Belgium, was a technically advanced, industrial region, while the Flanders part was predominantly agricultural. *[Both Wallonia and Flanders are in Belgium.]* After WW II this difference between Wallonia and Flanders faded because Belgium had its industrial infrastructure relatively intact, and this set the stage for rapid development, particularly in Flanders. Belgium was saved from destruction because of the Galopin doctrine. Flanders was particularly poised to grow because it was very close to Antwerp, which is a big port in Europe. Also, Flanders improved because of the European Union and NATO in Brussels, also close to Flanders. The older and traditional industries in Wallonia began to lose their competitive edge during this period. However, because the world economy was growing, there were no immediate effects on Belgium's economy, at least not until 1973. Unfortunately, the oil price shocks from 1973 to 1979 and the resultant demand and supply equation of oil brought the Belgian economy into a period of protracted recession *(economic slump)*.

All this contributed to Wallonia losing its primacy, and Flanders growing in importance for Belgium. In the 1980s and 1990s, the economic progress of the country started resulting from Flanders. In the early 1980s, Belgium faced a difficult period of structural adjustment caused by declining demand for its traditional products, its worsening economic performance, and neglected structural reform. Consequently, the recession from 1980-82 devastated Belgium in many ways—unemployment rose, social welfare costs increased, personal debt rose, the government deficit touched 13% of GDP, and the national debt, although mostly held domestically, thrived. This was the time for quick and effective action. Against this slump, in 1982, Prime Minister Martens' government formulated an economic recovery program to promote export-led growth by enhancing the competitiveness of Belgium's export industries. As a result, economic growth rose from 2% in 1984 to a peak of 4% in 1989. In May 1990, the government linked the Belgian currency, the franc, to the German currency, the mark. However, as German interest rates rose after 1990, Belgian rates increased following it and resulted in a decline in the economic growth rate of Belgium again.

Belgium, otherwise a wealthy country, had spent more but collected less taxes for years. Belgium reacted to the 1973 and 1979 oil price hikes with poor macroeconomic policies: it absorbed the workers who were laid off in the private sector into the public sector and subsidized sick industries—coal, steel, textiles, glass, and shipbuilding—in order to support the economy. But due to this, debt reached 121% of GNP by the end of the 1980s. However, thanks to Belgium's high personal savings rate, the Belgian Government managed to finance the deficit mainly from domestic savings. This minimized the damaging effects on the overall economy.

The economy of Belgium is influenced by regional differences, and is varied. The Flemish (referring to Flanders) and Walloon (referring to Wallonia) economies differ. Productivity in Flanders is 20% higher per person. While the Brussels GDP is higher than the Flemish or Walloon GDP, this is misleading because the people who work in Brussels (contributing to its GDP) actually live in Flanders or Wallonia. Unemployment in Wallonia is higher than it is in Flanders. Unemployment is the highest in Brussels.

The passage is about the devastated economy of Belgium and how it rose after WWII. Flanders, part of Belgium, led the growth of Belgium, but the oil price shock from 1973-79 pushed Belgium into an extended period of slump. During the early 80s, it faced many economic challenges from structural adjustment caused by low demand of its products, and poor economic performance. In 1982, PM Martens started an economic recovery program led by export-oriented growth. Economic growth rose from 2% to 4% in 1989. In 1990, the government linked the Belgian currency (the franc) to the German currency (the mark), but the move resulted in a decline in the economic growth rate. The author blames Belgium's damaged economy on the fact that Belgium reacted to the 1973 and 1979 oil price hikes with poor macroeconomic policies: it supported and subsidized sick industries. Due to this, debt reached 121% of GNP by the end of the 80s. The author ends the passage on a positive note, saying that the Belgian economy could finance the deficit mainly from domestic savings it had accrued over the years, which minimized the damaging effects on the overall economy.

Main Point: Surmounting the challenges of the devastated Belgian economy through structural reforms after WWII.

Question 1-Solution

This is a main point question from the general category.

(A) This option is **incorrect** because the passage is not about Flanders and its rising to take a leadership position in Belgium, but about the Belgian economy.

(B) This is the **correct** answer because the passage discusses the Belgian economy under structural readjustment. This option correctly addresses the challenges the Belgian economy had to face after WWII.

(C) This option is **incorrect** because the passage only mentions P.M. Martens as influencing economic restructuring; this option only narrowly covers the scope of the passage.

(D) This option is **incorrect** because the topic of the passage is not just the damage inflicted by the government.

The correct answer is B.

Question 2-Solution

This is a function question.

(A) This option is **incorrect** because the passage does not demonstrate how all of Belgium could have followed Flanders's example in order to prevent economic hardship. Flanders' rise after the war was coincidental, and not a deliberate plan that brought success.

(B) This is the **correct** answer because the success of Flanders in some sectors and the decline of Walloon in other sectors exemplifies the change in the economy as a whole.

(C) This option is **incorrect** because it is not demonstrated that Belgium was in a position to experience "runaway" economic growth. In fact, the damaged situation in the Belgian economy is being discussed throughout the passage.

(D) This option is **incorrect** because there is no single factor that drove away growth in the Belgian economy.

The correct answer is B.

Question 3 -Solution

This is a specific inference question.

(A) This option is **incorrect** because the oil price hikes were not a structural problem with the Belgian economy, but rather an outside event faced by the entire world.

(B) This option is **incorrect** because policymaking did not immediately change in response to the oil price hikes. Also, the author would not consider the eventual policy changes "an improvement" because he thinks that Belgium's response did not contain effective macroeconomic perspectives.

(C) This is the **correct** answer because the oil price hikes revealed the inherent weakness in Belgian economic organization and exposed it; such weakness in the economy was present all along but was not being revealed. This is comparable to the fable in which an emperor goes around without clothes and nobody dares to point it out, except a child. Thus, the analogy is that Belgium is analogous to the unclothed emperor and the oil price hikes are similar to the child who pointed out *(revealed)* that the emperor *(Belgium's economy)* had no clothes *(was weak)*.

(D) This option is **incorrect** because the precarious Belgian economic condition preceded the oil price hikes. Belgian economy was not in great shape before the oil price hikes. Only Flanders' rise and the world economy kept it going.

The correct answer is C.

Question 4 -Solution

This is a specific inference question.

(A) This option is **incorrect** because the passage does not consider Martens' efforts to be misspent. He managed to bring Belgium up a bit.

(B) This is the **correct** answer because the passage seeks to show that the progress Martens made was amid genuine economic difficulty even if it lacked macroeconomic perspective.

(C) This option is **incorrect** because the passage does credit Martens with improving aspects of the Belgian economy. Also, the author does criticize Martens' lack of macroeconomic perspective.

(D) This option is **incorrect** because the Belgian economy did improve after a bad run.

The correct answer is B.

Question 5-Solution

This is a tone question from the general category.

(A)   This is the **correct** answer because it is providing a historical interpretation of the actions taken during a period.

(B)   This option is **incorrect** because the passage does not seek to assert a political position or discuss a controversy.

(C)   This option is **incorrect** because the passage does not seek to argue against an interpretation of the facts.

(D)   This option is **incorrect** because the passage is better understood as a historical interpretation rather than as all-encompassing account of events.

The correct answer is A.

Question 6-Solution

This is an inference question.

(A)   This option is **incorrect** because the passage mentions ways in which the government responded advantageously using its power.

(B)   This is the **correct** answer because the passage suggests that it is economically inefficient to aid ailing industries. The author mentions that the subsidizing drove up the government's debt to 121% of GNP, suggesting that the author personally does not agree with this measure.

(C)   This option is **incorrect** because the passage does not accuse the government of making decisions too slowly.

(D)   This option is **incorrect** because the passage seeks to demonstrate the need to structure the economy in a way that is appropriate to minimize the effects of market fluctuation.

The correct answer is B.

Question 7 -Solution

This is an inference question.

(A)   This option is **incorrect** because the passage does not assert that economists are not pragmatists.

(B)   This is the **correct** answer because the piece is a historical interpretation and makes assessments of the correct course of action after the fact, which is different from making decisions at the time of issue.

(C)   This option is **incorrect** because the author does assert that correct answers cannot be found in economics.

(D)   This option is **incorrect** because the passage does not mention that the policy decisions were politically motivated.

The correct answer is B.

Question 8-Solution

This is a tone question from the general category.

(A) This is the **correct** answer because the passage acknowledges the advantages and disadvantages of high rates; the tone has traits of ambivalence. If the question asked us the tone towards "high personal savings alone" we could say that the passage is positively inclined towards it, but we cannot say it is either positive or negative about "high rates of interest".

(B) Like option B, this option is **incorrect** because the passage sees some advantages in high interest rates, so the author does not see it threatening.

(C) This option is tricky, but **incorrect**, though it may seem correct except for the concern expressed by the author regarding the slowing the Belgium economy. If the question asked us the tone towards "high personal savings alone" we could say that the passage is positively inclined towards it.

(D) This option is **incorrect** because the passage does not expect failure as the natural consequence of high interest rates, but acknowledges successes and difficulties.

The correct answer is A.

Question 9-Solution

The word "masked" is used in the sentence: *The older, traditional industries of Wallonia, particularly steelmaking, began to lose their competitive edge during this period, but the general growth of world prosperity **masked** this deterioration until the 1973 and 1979 oil price shocks and resultant shifts in international demand sent the economy into a period of prolonged recession.*

From the sentence, we can deduce that though a few traditional industries in Wallonia started declining, the general growth of world prosperity offset the ill-effects on the Belgian economy. In other words, we can say that *the general growth of world prosperity* helped the poor state of a few traditional industries of Wallonia remain unexposed, or concealed the deterioration. Thus, option A is the correct answer.

Other options do not qualify for the replacement of "masked", as perplexed means confused– not apt in meaning in this context; eluded means escaped/dodged–inappropriate in the given context; and deceived means cheated–again an improper word in this context.

The correct answer is A.

Question 10-Solution

We have been asked to choose a sentence that furnishes evidence for the statement explaining Flanders' climb over Wallonia. Thus, the sentence must explain why Flanders overtook Wallonia after WWI.

Let's analyze the options one by one.

(A)   This option is **incorrect** because the sentence *"For 200 years until World War I, French-speaking Wallonia was a technically advanced, industrial region, while Dutch-speaking Flanders was predominantly agricultural with very little industrial work, mainly processing agricultural products and making textiles"* discusses the opposite of what we need. This sentence shows Wallonia's primacy over Flanders, and not the other way round.

(B)   This option is **incorrect** because the sentence *"This disparity began to fade during the interwar period"* is too general and does not contain any hard evidence.

(C)   This option is **correct** because the sentence *"The institution of the European Union and NATO in Brussels improved the state of industry in Flanders greatly, given its proximity to Antwerp, which is the second-largest port in Europe after Rotterdam"* provides data on what made Flanders gain ground on Wallonia.

(D)   This option is **incorrect** because even though the sentence *"The older, traditional industries of Wallonia, particularly steelmaking, began to lose their competitive edge during this period, but the general growth of world prosperity masked this deterioration until the 1973 and 1979 oil price shocks and resultant shifts in international demand sent the economy into a period of prolonged recession"* contains discussions of the falling behind of Wallonia, it does not explain why Flanders gained ground.

The correct answer is C.

Question 11-Solution

This is a reasoning question.

We have been asked to find out something that would reduce Brussels' GDP, according to the information in the passage. This information is provided in the final paragraph, which states that Brussels' GDP is higher than that of Flanders and that of Wallonia, but this is artificial because the people who work in Brussels (contributing to its GDP) actually live in Flanders or Wallonia. Thus, to reduce Brussels' GDP, we just need to calculate GDP according to people's home address and not according to their place of work; that is, calculate GDP of a place by the contribution of people who live there.

Let's analyze the options one by one.

(A)   This option is **incorrect** because this is what the status quo is. Currently Brussels GDP is calculated on the basis of people who work there, so GDP will remain unaffected.

(B)   This option is **incorrect** because this is out of scope. The passage does not discuss the ways Flanders and Wallonia calculate their GDPs.

(C)   This option is **incorrect** because of the same reasoning used in option A. This is what the status quo is.

(D)   This option is **correct** because this matches our deductions above.

The correct answer is D.

7.4   Passage 4 (Craving for fast food: whom to blame: behavior or the brain?)

Understanding the Passage

This is a medium length passage of medium difficulty level on medical science and human behavior.

The passage presents a graph that shows that obesity is increasing. A finding from scientists has shown that consuming more "fast food" *(food with a high content of processed sugar, salt, and saturated fats)* can be addictive like other controlled substances *(heroin, narcotics, etc.)*. According to researchers, "fast food" can trigger an addiction in the brain asking for more "fast food". *[Scientists conclude that 'fast food' is addictive and it demands regular feeding.]*. Many scientists see a relationship between people's decisions to choose "fast food" as their preferred food and influencing factors in the environmental such as the wide availability of "fast foods". *[The scientists believe that people want to eat fast food mainly because of a permissive culture, the environment, and the easy availability of fast food]*; it leads to detrimental effects on human health and development. The researchers conclude that the brains of overeaters of fast foods experience some chemical changes triggering more appetite for the unhealthy food. *[The scientists believe that as one starts eating fast food regularly, the brain undergoes changes and craves more and more fast food.]*

If people continue to eat too much unhealthy food, it will initiate changes in the brain that raise the minimum level of eating the brain is usually satisfied with. *[Eating addictive stuff, or fast food, follows the law of diminishing returns, i.e. the amount that one needs to eat to get satisfied keeps increasing over time.]* Moreover, high consumption of "fast foods" stimulates opiate receptors in the brain *[opiate receptors are distributed widely in the brain; they act as natural pain relievers and eating fast food mimics this effect.)*. Due to this, frequent and bigger doses of "fast food" feign some effects of opiates. *[Scientists contend that an uncontrolled diet of unhealthy food makes changes in the brain's response. The brain is only satisfied with bigger and more frequent meals. Since the effect of fast food is similar to that of opiates, or pain relievers, people crave more to get the same psychotropic effect.]*. Scientists performed an experiment on rats. They fed rats on a sugar-rich diet; when they stopped the sugar-rich diet, they found that the rats showed the symptoms of withdrawal— shivering and chattering teeth. Their behavior was comparable to opiate addicts when the supply of opium is reduced to such addicts. When the rats were given drugs that block opiate receptors *(natural pain releiving substance in brain)*, the dopamine levels in their brains *(an area linked with the dynamics of reward—reward is used for "craving for more food" and responsible for keeping a person addicted)* looked similar to those in heroin addicts. The scientists concluded that obesity can be viewed as a disease beyond the control of those affected by it *(just as addiction is beyond the control of addicts)*. *[Scientists contend that the propensity to eat more unhealthy food and get fatter is not truly related to one's behavior, but rather to changes in the neurochemistry of the brain.]*

Lawyers argue that society has a responsibility to regulate food and educate people about the abuse of "unhealthy foods". Fast food companies should be held accountable for the ill-effects arising from unhealthy food. Some scientists are still skeptical about the degree to which some researchers attribute the addiction of unhealthy food to be the cause of neurological disorder, rather than people's behavior being the cause. *(Some skeptics think that it is not right to blame neurochemistry alone for fast food addiction. People choose to eat fast food and so choice should be accountable too.)* They contend that a habit and an addiction can be differentiated on qualitative parameters and not on quantitative parameters. *[These scientists think that some people habitually eat fast food but never overeat while others overeat fast food repeatedly, and this difference is not just the quantity of fast food consumed by both.]* The scientists think it's a qualitative difference, i.e. the qualities of these people differ. Not all who eat fast food regularly throw caution to the wind and eat all they want, but those who become addicted overrule common sense and eat more than is justified. These scientists think we cannot blame neurochemistry changes alone for differences between habitual fast food eaters and addicted overeaters.

The author cites a finding made by a few scientists claiming that unhealthy food, if consumed regularly and in large proportions, will make some neurological disorder in the brain which in turn causes the brain to ask for more food to satiate it. This leads to ill-effects such as obesity. They contend that obesity cannot be tackled only with exercising discipline in eating, as the brain will not be satisfied and will ask for more such food. It needs to be treated like any other addiction disease. Some scientists are skeptical as to the degree of this claim.

The author negates the scientists who suggest that obesity is based on lack of discipline in making personal choices. He states that those scientists do not take into account that choices are not independently made but are influenced. The obesity epidemic is not caused by overeating healthy foods, but by overeating sugars and fats, both of which are easy to produce on a mass-scale. Such production suitability allows manufacturers to flood the market and surroundings with foods full of these unhealthy substances, thereby deeply influencing the food choices that people make, proving that choices are not independent. Also, such foods have been proven to be addictive and simply advocating a disciplined approach won't work.

Also, if personal choice is kept as the main reason, the government would have no need to take any responsibility or actions. Then factors such as advertising, lack of menu labelling, and the addictive properties of industrial food will remain unchanged and keep impacting people's food choices. Even economics suggests that the government must intervene when the market fail to take care of people's health. To change this grim scenario, simply changing policies is not enough. Deeper measures will need to be taken.

Main Point: Addiction to unhealthy food is triggered more by the brain and less by undisciplined behavior, but some scientists remain unconvinced.

Question 1-Solution

This is an inference question.

(A) This is the **correct** answer because the passage demonstrates that people can be affected by environmental influences that create a cycle of addiction, though they may not be aware that chemical imbalance may have unconsciously affected their decision-making.

(B) This option is **incorrect** because the passage makes a distinction between being vulnerable to a cycle of addiction and having no responsibility over one's own behavior for an eating disorder. The passage does not suggest that overeaters are not responsible for their behavior. It just states that overeaters cannot control their impulse to overeat because their neurochemistry is affected. However, they still remain responsible for what's happening to them. They need to be treated like any other addict.

(C) This option may be correct, but it is not affirmed in the passage. It's out of scope.

(D) This option is **incorrect** because the passage does not say that overeaters are unable to overcome the difficulties of withdrawal. It does not even suggest that they try to withdraw from it.

The correct answer is A.

Question 2 -Solution

This is an inference question.

(A) This option is **incorrect** because there is a relationship between these two factors, but other things could influence dopamine levels, so those levels are not necessarily dependent on whether drugs are administered. This does not heed the rule of the option that "must be true".

(B) This option is **incorrect** because the relationship is not presented in the passage as being directly correlated. It is a tricky but an extreme option. 'Directly correlated' means that two variables move in tandem; however we cannot infer this from the passage.

(C) This is the **correct** answer because there is a relationship between administering drugs and dopamine levels, implying that they are related.

(D) This option is **incorrect** because they are related.

The correct answer is C.

Question 3 -Solution

This is reasoning based question on strengthening the argument.

(A) This option is **incorrect** because the argument is vulnerable to criticism; even if obesity is a pre-existing condition in individuals, companies are still responsible for protecting consumers from possible side effects that the consumers may experience because of a company's products.

(B) This option is **incorrect** because corporations are expected to provide consumers with a safe product or to warn them of its dangers. Arguing that obese people must treat their disease with medication that blocks opiate receptors is akin to shirking responsibility.

(C) This is the **correct** answer because it eliminates the threat of an addiction caused by the product by establishing that obesity is a result of consumer habits, not addiction to products. This will prove that overeating is not a result of neurochemistry-altering effects of the company's products. This option will put the responsibility on the consumer *(by implying that moderation is a choice)* and free the company from the blame of making addictive products.

(D) This option is **incorrect** because corporations are still liable for the unforeseen damage caused by their products, even if they have only just now learned that "fast food" causes chemical dependency in people. This will not free them from blame.

The correct answer is C.

Question 4 -Solution

This is a function question.

(A)   This option is **incorrect** because while it may be true, the purpose of the scientists, as presented in the passage, is not to argue about strict diets.

(B)   This option is **incorrect** because it is not necessarily true. Even those who are not obese can be equally vulnerable to the health hazards of the chronic consumption of "fast food". The passage does not support such a deduction.

(C)   This is the **correct** answer because treating obesity as a disease allows people to understand that obese people suffer from their behavior in a way that people without the disease may not. There are factors other than individual behavior, such as chemical imbalance, solely considered responsible for obesity. The scientists do think that environmental factors and neurochemistry changes are responsible for obesity.

(D)   This option is **incorrect** because it is not true and is not stated by the scientists mentioned in the passage.

The correct answer is C.

Question 5 -Solution

This is a detail question.

(A)   This is the **correct** answer because the researchers object to the conclusions reached based on the evidence *(findings)* of their colleagues. *(Refer to the first sentence of the passage.)* The skeptics believe that the data may exist on neurochemistry being altered but the extent to which individual choices determine obesity should not be discounted. Thus the skeptics disagree with the conclusion of the researchers.

(B)   This option is **incorrect** because there is no mention in the passage that suggests that the researchers doubted the expertise of their colleagues. They certainly were skeptical about the findings presented by their colleagues, but the passage did not allude to doubts on their expertise.

(C)   This option is **incorrect** because there is no mention of the proponents making any assumptions that the skeptics disagreed on.

(D)   This option is **incorrect** because there is no mention of the method, nor of the opponents' objection to it in the passage.

The correct answer is A.

Question 6 -Solution

This is a function question.

(A)   This option is **incorrect** because the skeptics do not disagree that overeaters are addicted. However, they object to the blame for the addiction being laid solely on chemical changes and not on individual choices.The dissenting scientists do not object to the way diseases are categorized.

(B)   This option is **incorrect** because the scientists mentioned in the beginning of the passage acknowledge that there are several factors that contribute to a person's behavior.

(C)   This is the **correct** answer because opponents view "qualitative" consumption choices to be primarily behavioral, and not primarily chemical, problems. So, it follows that those skeptics would object to the assumption that addictive behavior has nothing to do with behavior and choices, and is dependent only on chemical imbalances in the brain.

(D)   This option is **incorrect** because this assumption is not made in the passage.

The correct answer is C.

Question 7 -Solution

This is a detail question.

(A)   This option is **incorrect** because dopamine makes rats happier as they pursue consumption (reward) and therefore they feel encouraged to eat more. Refer to the latter part of the second paragraph: "*Later, by treating rats with drugs that block opiate receptors, scientists were able to lower the amount of dopamine in the nucleus acumen of rats' brains, an area linked with the dynamics of reward.*" The word "reward" is used here for "more food". It can be inferred that by lowering the level of dopamine, the desire for more food reduces, so the role of dopamine would be to long for more food (and to reward oneself).

(B)   This option is **incorrect** because dopamine does not block opiates. The passage talked about opiate-blocking drugs that helped to lower dopamine levels.

(C)   This option is **incorrect** because, on the contrary, dopamine is linked to the reward mechanism, which activates when rats receive opiates.

(D)   This is the **correct** answer since rats are encouraged to eat more. It follows from the deduction made in option A's explanation.

The correct answer is D.

Question 8 -Solution

This is an inference question.

(A)   This option is **incorrect** because we cannot infer from the passage that the lawyers' position implies that the government lacks knowledge.

(B)   This is the **correct** answer because the passage states that lawyers argue that there is 'a responsibility to regulate food and educate people about the abuse of "unhealthy foods" in a way that is comparable to society's control of opiates and narcotics. Corporations ("fast food" restaurants) that target this vulnerability (addiction to "fast food") in human beings can then be held liable. . .'

(C)   This option is **incorrect** because lawyers are arguing that it is the responsibility of corporations, and not the market, to keep consumers informed and to compensate for damage caused by their products.

(D)   This option is **incorrect** because by placing the responsibility of a good diet on the individual, the lawyers' objective to make "fast food" restaurants liable will get diluted.

The correct answer is B.

Question 9 -Solution

This is a reasoning question.

We need to strengthen the argument made in the fourth paragraph. In the fourth paragraph, the author argues that fast food is indeed addictive, and advocating discipline is not a solution to such addiction. Thus, any option that reinforces that obesity is caused not by personal choice or lack of discipline, but by the overwhelming presence of unhealthy food, will strengthen this claim.

Let's analyze the options one by one.

(A)   This option is **correct** because this matches our deductions above. It shows that when food choices available are healthy, people make healthy choices, thereby proving that available food options influence choices, not discipline or lack of it.

(B)   This option is **incorrect** because this option is irrelevant to proving our point. Feelings are irrelevant by themselves to proving that discipline is not an issue in obesity.

(C)   This option is **incorrect** because this option, too, would not prove any point, neither about discipline nor about surroundings.

(D)   This option is **incorrect** because it may support the claim that discipline can undo obesity, thereby suggesting that obesity is a matter of lack of discipline and not influenced by surroundings or choices. This would weaken the claim.

The correct answer is A.

Chart for questions # 10 & 11

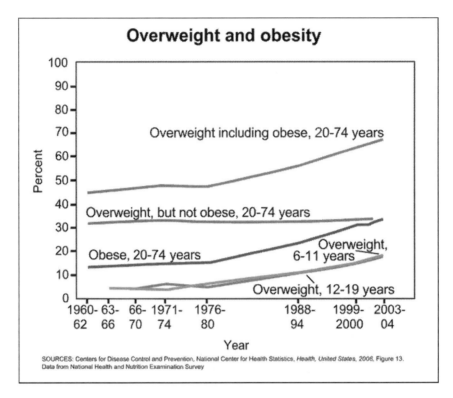

Question 10 -Solution

Note that this is question in which we have to choose an option that is not supported by the passage; it means that three statements would be supported by the passage.

Let us analyze each option one by one.

(A) Note that we must look at the second line from the top of the graph: **Overweight, but not obese, 20-74 years.** We see that the line curve is pretty straight and in fact there is a slight dip after 1971, so the option statement, in fact, is wrong. It's the opposite. So this is the **correct** answer. Though we have the correct answer, let's discuss the other options for the sake of understanding.

(B) This statement is supported by the graph. Post 1980, for the age group 6-11, as well as for the age group 12-19, the line curve for the percentage of those who are overweight has ascended, thus we can conclude that percentage of those who are overweight for the age group 6-19 has risen significantly.

(C) Refer to the third line down from the top. We see that for the period 1960-80, the line curve, though it has slightly ascended, is not as steep as for the period 1980-2004. Thus the statement is supported by the passage.

(D) This statement is also supported by the passage. We see that both the line curves are overlapping each other for that period, thus the increase in percentage of those who are overweight is almost the same.

The correct answer is A.

Question 11 -Solution

Let us analyze each option one by one.

(A)   This is **correct** answer because the two lines at the bottom, representing youngsters, lie far below the flat line representing adults (20-74).

(B)   This is **incorrect** because the graph suggests that from 1960-80, in the age group 20-74, the percentage of people who are **overweight, but not obese** is fewer than 50%. Refer to the top of the graph. The line, in fact, breaches the 50% mark in 1980-88.

(C)   This is **incorrect** because we cannot deduce the characteristics of a sub-group (age group 30-50) from the characteristics of a parent group (age-group 20-74). The line for the age group 20-74 is the average of all people falling between the ages of 20 and 74, and there may be significant deviations in the characteristics of these people.

(D)   This is **incorrect** because the graph does not provide line curves for those who are **obese** for the age group 6-11 and for the age group 12-19.

The correct answer is A.

7.5   Passage 5 (Gas attacks during the World Wars)

Understanding the Passage

This is a short passage of low difficulty level on wartime history.

Poison gas was the scariest warfare tactic in WWI. It was indiscriminate (not methodical, needing no special aim) and could be used even when actual firing and fighting were not going on. What made poison gas so scary and harmful was that death from poison gas was long-drawn, painful, and agonizing, unlike death from guns and bullets, which was almost instant. Furthermore, soldiers could seek shelter from bullets inside trenches, but nothing other than crude gas masks was available as defense against poison gas. Even though using gas was frowned upon, France used it against Germany. However, Germans used gas in a detailed and developed manner, causing severe damage during the war. An info-graphic is presented containing details of the specific gases employed and the effects of those gases.

World War II exposed America to the vulnerability of the security of its citizens. Unlike in WW II, in WW I the citizens were never attacked, and so during WW II, nations were not prepared for attack on civilian populations. Every nation used this tactic (of attacking civilians) to try to gain the upper hand in the war. Examples of Germany and Britain using this war tactic are mentioned in the passage.

The highest priority for America was the protection of children from possible attack. WW II had a history of participating nations attacking civilian areas. It was started by Germany on London, and then the Allied Forces retaliated with attack on the German city of Dresden.

A leading concern for Britain and the U.S. was the exposure to gas attack upon the unaware youth population, especially in urban areas (because urban areas have denser populations). Immediately after Pearl Harbor (a completely unexpected attack by Japan on Hawaii, a US territory), thousands of military training masks were rushed (by the US government) to people living on the islands (of the U.S.) as preventive measures against gas attacks. However, these masks were unsuitable for protecting children. Hawaiian officials produced an expedient (self-serving) made up of bunny ears and a hood. The Sun Rubber Company designed a relatively acceptable mask based on the universal Walt Disney cartoon figure Mickey Mouse. The adoption of these masks made them popular among children; this, in turn, potentially reduced the element of fear with the masks. (So, the author implies that the first masks were unsuitable for children because the children probably did not wear them out of fear or annoyance. Hence, disguising the masks by associating them with fun elements could convince children to wear those gas masks.)

This measure would increase the chances of survival of the youth population. It was important to protect the youth because large numbers of working age males were vulnerable to losing their lives fighting overseas. (Children and youth comprised an important part of the population because most of the able-bodied working males were posted as soldiers fighting in the war, and many could die, leaving the country without a productive population.)

Here, the passage discusses the mechanism of protecting the youth population of the US from possible gas attacks during WW II. The author discusses the importance of protecting them, the challenges with masks, and the popularity and adoption of innovatively designed masks for children.

The chief user of gas warfare was Germany, then France, followed by Britain. The number of fatalities from poison gas is debatable because its impact is difficult to measure, but the terror it caused was unmistakable.

Poison gas led to 188,000 casualties (injuries) among the British, of which 8,100 were fatal (causing death). Russia was thought to have the maximum number of fatalities from poison gas (over 50,000). France suffered 8,000 fatalities due to poison gas. In total, there were about 1,250,000 gas-related injuries, of which 91,000 were fatal (less than 10% were fatal), with over 50% of these fatalities being Russian. However, these figures do not take into account the number of men who died from poison gas-related injuries years after the end of the war; nor do they take into account the number of men who survived, but were so badly incapacitated by poison gas that they could hold down no job once they had been released by the army. (Thus, the actual impact is far higher than the calculated numbers.)

Main Point: The use of poison gas and the mechanism to protect youth from gas attacks during WW II, along with the challenges associated with that.

Question 1-Solution

This is a detail question.

The second paragraph of the passage mentions that World War II exposed America to problems with the security of its citizens. Unlike in WW II, in WW I the citizens were never attacked. Option D is the only answer mentioned in the passage distinguishing World War I from World War II.

The correct answer is D.

Question 2 -Solution

This is a function question.

(A) This option is **incorrect** because no such intent of destroying the civilian wartime infrastructure was reflected in the passage.

(B) Like option A, this option is **incorrect** because there was no mention of reducing the number of potential reinforcements for dwindling armies in the passage.

(C) This option is **incorrect** because nothing of this sort was stated in the passage.

(D) This is the **correct** answer, as stated in the sentence: "Germany unleashed the lengthiest bombing campaign of the war on the people of London primarily to weaken British morale."

The correct answer is D.

Question 3 -Solution

This is a detail question.

Option C is supported by the last section of the passage. *"The popularity of these masks was dependent on internalizing their use in children ...This potentially reduced the element of fear. If the element of fear could be diminished, gas masks might be employed by their owners more quickly in the event of an attack, and also worn without interruption."*

The design of gas masks to look like Mickey Mouse was intended to encourage children to wear the masks, and wear them properly, so that they were safe against possible gas attacks.

Other options are either not supported by the passage, or irrelevant.

The correct answer is C.

Question 4 -Solution

This is an inference question

Option C is indicated by the sentence in the last paragraph *"All of this would increase the chances of survival of the youth population, of no small concern to a nation with large numbers of its working age males facing the perils of combat overseas."*

In other words, the measure of protecting children from possible gas attacks would increase the chances of survival of the youth population; it is important to protect the youth because a large number of working age males were vulnerable to losing their lives fighting overseas.

Other options are either not supported by the passage or irrelevant.

The correct answer is C.

Question 5 -Solution

This is a detail question.

Even if you do not know its meaning, you can figure it out from the context. The word is used here: *"However, the available equipment was unsuitable for protecting children. Instead, Hawaiian officials produced an* expedient *made up of bunny ears and a hood. This would lead to further improvisation in the protection of the child civilian population."*

From the context, we can at least understand that Hawaiian officials must have produced something to address a problem.
Let us analyze the options one by one.

(A)   This is **incorrect** because "expedient" is used to address a problem, whereas the meaning of "a dire consequence" is to face a negative repercussion.

(B)   This is **incorrect** because in order to protect children, it is absurd to assume that Hawaiian officials would offer a cleaning agent.

(C)   This is the **correct** answer because an "expedient" is something self-serving, helpful, or useful in a particular situation.

(D)   This is **incorrect** because with the same reasoning used in option B, in order to protect children, it is absurd to assume that Hawaiian officials would teach a terror tactic.

The correct answer is C.

Question 6-Solution

This is a function question.

Option D is correct since the passage states: *"The popularity of these masks was dependent on internalizing their use in children by making their presence part of a perceived game. This potentially reduced the element of fear that the masks conveyed on their recipients. If the element of fear could be diminished, gas masks might be employed by their owners more quickly in the event of an attack ..."*

Other options are either not supported by the passage or irrelevant.

The correct answer is D.

Question 7 -Solution

This is an Inference question.

(A)   This option is **incorrect** because the youth of the civilian population itself is not the danger.

(B)   This is the **correct** answer since the point of providing gas masks in a familiar form is to allow civilians to make the correct decisions by being prepared to act correctly. This implies that civilians sometimes do not wear masks even when they know that they are in danger. Thus, the government felt the urge to design masks that would be appealing and would be worn.

(C)   This option is **incorrect** because it is not supported by the passage. Though the mention of the attack of Germany on Britain was meant to weaken British morale, the author did not ratify it as a significant avoidable danger of a wartime terror attack. Also, we cannot necessarily conclude that this is an avoidable danger. It does not depend on the country itself, but on the attacking country.

(D)   This option is **incorrect** because it is not supported by the passage, and lack of warning of an attack is not an avoidable danger.

The correct answer is B.

Question 8 -Solution

We have to choose a sentence that provides evidence for the claim that attack from poison gas was more feared than any other attack. Thus, we need a sentence that discusses other attacks and their effect on soldiers, and poison attack and its effect.

Let's analyze the options one by one.

(A)   This option is **incorrect** because the sentence "*WWI introduced the scariest attack weapon – poison gas.*" is too generic and does not provide any evidence why poison gas was feared more than any other attack.

(B)   This option is **incorrect** because the sentence "*It was ruthless, and random. It could be used even when actual fighting was not going on*", too, is generic and does not discuss why poison gas was feared more than any other attack.

(C)   This option is **incorrect** because this sentence "*However, these figures do not take into account the number of men who died from poison gas-related injuries years after the end of the war; nor do they take into account the number of men who survived but were so badly incapacitated by poison gas that they could hold down no job once they had been released by the army*" provides proof that poison gas caused more damage than can be calculated, but not why it was feared more than any other attack. The correct sentence must include a comparative description of why gas attacks scared soldiers more than any other attack.

(D)   This option is **correct** because the sentence "*The machines guns wounded and killed far more soldiers but soldiers could seek shelter from guns in the trenches and even if they did not, death was instant, whereas poison gas caught soldiers unawares and death was slow and excruciatingly painful, dragging on for days with no relief until it sapped the courage of people around the afflicted*" provides proof why poison gas attacks were feared more than any other attack.

The correct answer is D.

Question 9 -Solution

This is a reasoning question.

We have to draw a conclusion from the final two paragraphs, which state that the actual impact of poison gas is debatable. While specific numbers of fatalities and casualties are recorded, the actual number of impacted people is much higher because certain effects of poison gas were not taken into account in calculating those numbers.

Let's analyze the options one by one.

(A)   This option is **incorrect** because while the passage states that poison gas attacks were feared more than any other, the penultimate paragraph states that the number of fatalities was relatively few - even if the terror impact did not diminish for the duration of the war.

(B) This option is **incorrect** because the penultimate paragraph states only that the impact of tanks is difficult to calculate, but not that it is negligible. This cannot be deduced from the paragraphs.

(C) This option is **correct** because this matches our deductions above.

(D) This option is **incorrect** because what the author feels about the morality of the use of poison gas, or even of the war itself, is not inferable from the passage.

The correct answer is C.

Chart for questions # 10 & 11

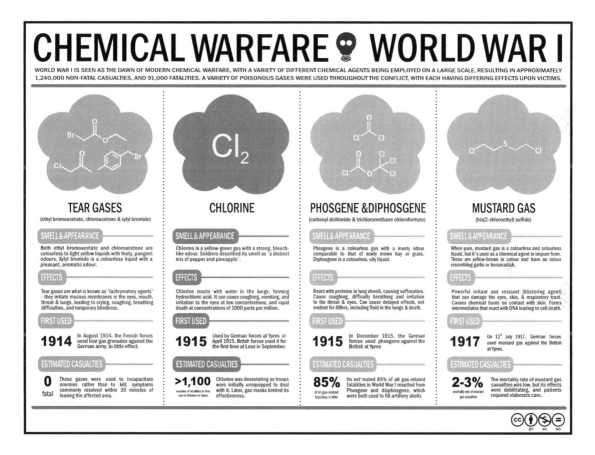

Question 10 -Solution

We have to find out a gas which a person would not have been aware of, but which caused fatality. A gas which has properties of being colorless, odorless, and fatal would be the answer. Colorless gas would be difficult to detect, and, thus, a person would be least aware of it, while an odorless gas is difficult to sense and plan an escape from.

Tear gas is **incorrect**, as it has pungent odor, but is not a fatal gas.

Chlorine gas is **incorrect** because it has a color and an odor.

Phosgene gas is **correct** because it is colorless, and while it has an odor, the odor is that of freshly cut grass), and thus it would not cause much alarm or seem threatening, making the gas difficult to beware of.

Impure mustard gas is an **incorrect** answer as it is neither colorless nor odorless, but it is fatal.

The correct option is C.

Question 11 -Solution

We have to find out the element which, if unavailable, would hamper the production of the maximum number of gases. So, we need the element which is present in the maximum number of gases.

Let's analyze the chemical formula and structure of every gas.

Tear gas: ethyl bromoacetate, chloro acetone and xylyl bromide – Elements: bromine, *chlorine*, oxygen (can be seen in the diagram)

Chlorine gas: Element – *chlorine*

Phosgene and Diphosgene gas: carbonyl dichloride, trichloromethane chloroformate: Elements – oxygen, *chlorine*

Mustard gas: 2-chloroethyl sulfide: Elements – sulfur, *chlorine*

From the analysis above, we can see that chlorine is an element present in all the gases. Thus, the unavailability of chlorine would hamper production of all the gases.

The correct option is B.

7.6   Passage 6 (Lord Dalhousie's uniform rate of postage in India)

Understanding the Passage

This is a short passage of low difficulty level on the topic of business sociology.

Lord Dalhousie introduced many reforms in his eight years as Governor General. His reforms seem to have been geared at creating a network of communication within India. He got the main places connected to the ports through railways, done not by money from the Indian treasury, but by the Government Guarantee method. Railways enhanced business and united India.

Dalhousie also introduced the telegraph in India, by which people could send messages easily. Additionally, Dalhousie established a separate department of public works to focus on development. Earlier, a military board was in charge of civil construction but it focused only on military work. With Dalhousie's change, the public works department worked extensively to improve irrigation, roads, and even colleges, among other things.

However, the most important reform that Lord Dalhousie is credited with was the creation of the modern postal system in India. He implemented the scheme of levying a uniform rate of postage throughout India, irrespective of origin or destination.

Many critics ridiculed Dalhousie's idea. It was, they said, pushing Rowland Hill's scheme of a penny postage for England to the extreme in India. They viewed it as a "reductio ad absurdum" of the reform that had been effected in Great Britain. [*It was termed extreme, as the area of India was far more than that of England. They implied a uniform rate was devoid of any logic; it was absurd!*].

Lord Dalhousie was firm in his decision to levy a uniform rate of postage. Prior to this, there used be an argument over the payment for delivery of every letter, and the rural postman used to charge additional money to the recipient for his service. But Dalhousie's intention was that, with the new simplistic system of postage stamps, petty bickering with postmen would cease to exist, and people would be assured of reliable service.

His postal system became a self-sustaining organization, due to which the outlay of finances for the postal service could be pruned. The social results were even more important. It has been said that the half-penny postage scheme by Lord Dalhousie was more significant in bridging the gap between the various parts of India than by earlier modes such as the telegraph, the railway, and other formal systems.

The passage is about the implementation of Lord Dalhousie's innovative but seemingly absurd postal scheme in India, which proposed to charge a uniform rate of postage thought India, irrespective of origin or destination. The passage talks about its success owing to its simplicity, and the social benefit it nurtured. A quote was given to highlight the importance of the postal reform by Dalhousie, stating that improving the postal system did far more than any other thing to improve life in India.

Main Point: Reforms by Dalhousie and the success of Lord Dalhousie's uniform rate of postal service scheme in India.

Question 1-Solution

This is a detail question.

Option A is the correct answer and is demonstrated by the description in the passage of the perceived injustice which opponents saw in the new Indian post system. Lord Dalhousie implemented the scheme of levying a uniform rate of postage throughout India, irrespective of origin or destination, which was ridiculed by many critics. It seemed absurd and unfair to charge the same amount for a letter going a long distance as one would charge for a letter going a short distance.

Though option B deserves a thought, it can be inferred from the passage that the proposed postal scheme by Lord Dalhousie was not unproven; it had been applied in England. Looking at the vast geographical area of India, however, it looked rather unfair. Also, the critics were opposed not because it was unproven, but because it seemed illogical.

Other options are either not discussed in the passage or are irrelevant.

The correct answer is A.

Question 2 -Solution

This is a detail question.

(A) This is the **correct** answer because in the last sentence of the passage, it was said that the half-penny postage scheme by Lord Dalhousie was more significant in bridging the gap between the various parts of India than by earlier modes such as the telegraph, the railway, and other formal systems. It adds "The social results were even more important." Thus, the system facilitated communication.

(B) This option is **incorrect** because it is not mentioned in the passage.

(C) This option is **incorrect** because though it was anticipated that the new postal system would be capable of putting a stop to corrupt methods of overcharging by postmen, it was not the prime benefit of the half-penny postal scheme in India.

(D) This option is **incorrect** because, though it was anticipated that the half-penny postal scheme in India would be self-sustainable and would not drain finances from the British colony to fund it, it was not the prime benefit to India. The passage says "The social results were even more important.", thus option A is the correct answer.

The correct answer is A.

Question 3 -Solution

This is an inference question.

(A) This option is **incorrect** because it is extreme and devoid of any solid reasoning.

(B)   This option is a close option, but **incorrect** because though the scheme succeeded in both places—the smaller one (England: a smaller geographical area compared to India), and the larger (India), we cannot infer that if something works on a small scale, it should work on a large scale as well, if executed properly. The statement focused on the "execution" whereas the "execution" of the scheme in India was not dealt with in detail in the passage.

(C)   This is the **correct** answer because the passage observes that benefits provided by uniform postage were the elimination of wrangling with local postman and the creation of reliability. If the result of these changes in the system was increased postage being sent, then the disorganization caused by the previous system may have been more costly than shipping a letter across India at a set rate, irrespective of cost. Thus, Dalhousie proved that charging uniform lower rates was a much better proposition in the longer term for the postal system than not.

(D)   This option is **incorrect** because it's out of scope.

The correct answer is C.

Question 4-Solution

This is an inference question.

(A)   This is the **correct** answer because it can be deduced from the experience of Dalhousie in different roles in the administration and internal development of the region, as well as his willingness to disregard the criticism of traditional financiers, whom we might assume were using traditional methods of problem resolution. He didn't see India's vastness as a detriment to the scheme that had worked in a smaller place successfully.

(B)   This option is **incorrect** because there is no evidence to support this.

(C)   This option is **incorrect** because there is no evidence to support this.

(D)   This option is **incorrect** because though the objective of bridging the gap between different parts of India was achieved through the postal scheme, other objectives could have been met through the telegraph, the railway, and public instruction, which were of equal importance.

The correct answer is A.

Question 5-Solution

This is a detail question.

Option C is the correct answer because **"reductio ad absurdum"** literally means to reduce something to an absurd degree, or to extend something to an absurd degree. However, if you are not sure about the meaning, you can still infer it from the context.

Let us examine the sentence and infer the meaning. *"For these onlookers, Dalhousie's plan was not so much an extension of the English penny postage scheme, as a **reductio ad absurdum** of the reform that had been effected in Great Britain."*

It is clear that the critics found the idea of implementing the postal scheme in India just because it had been a success in England absurd. They were of the opinion that extending the same scheme in a much larger place was inconceivable. Clearly option C is the correct answer.

The correct answer is C.

Question 6 -Solution

This is a detail question.

Option B is the correct answer, as indicated in the sentence stating: "The system was more reliable for the person mailing the letter, and encouraged **increased patronage**."

Other options are either not discussed in the passage or are irrelevant.

The correct answer is B.

Question 7-Solution

This is a detail question.

Option D can be seen as the correct answer from the sentence stating: "The proof of his success was the renewal of the postal system as a self-sustaining organization rather than its continuance as a chronic drain on British colonial finances."

Though option A may also seem to be correct, there is no evidence present in the passage to show increased patronage as a result of the scheme.

Other options are either not discussed in the passage or are irrelevant.

The correct answer is D.

Question 8 -Solution

This is an inference question.

(A)   This option is **incorrect** because, in fact, it is the other way around. A uniform rate of postage irrespective of distances shows that transaction costs may not increase substantially, even in larger markets.

(B)   This option is **incorrect** because it is an extreme answer. We cannot infer this from the passage.

(C)   This option is **incorrect** because it is an extreme answer. We cannot infer this from the passage. Though there was mention of postmen wrangling over the charges to deliver letters and squeeze some extra money from the recipient, calling them "always corrupt" is an extreme reaction.

(D) This is the **correct** answer because wrangling (disputing/bickering) with the local post-man appeared costly as it limited the reliability of the system. This unreliability decreased patronage and raised costs. However, when rates were standardized, patronage increased to the extent that the postal system became self-sustaining and did not need the British government's financial intervention. So, this can be inferred.

The correct answer is D.

Question 9 -Solution

We have been asked to find a statement that shows that the authorities were not necessarily in favor of the reforms put forth by Dalhousie. Thus, we need to show that the authorities were either unwilling, or needed to be persuaded, to allow some reforms.

Let's analyze the options one by one.

(A) This option is **incorrect** because the sentence "*The reforms introduced by Lord Dalhousie in India during his eight-year stint as the Governor General are many*" does not show any resistance from authorities to any reform; it is a general statement.

(B) This option is **correct** because the sentence "*Dalhousie **convinced** the authorities of the need of the railways and laid down the main lines of their development*" matches our deductions.

(C) This option is **incorrect** because the sentence "*Before Lord Dalhousie, military boards were in charge of the construction of public works*" does not show that the authorities were not willing to go along with any of Dalhousie's reforms.

(D) This option is **incorrect** because the sentence "*Dalhousie's special contribution was the construction of an engineering college at Roorkee and in other presidencies*" also does not show any resistance from authorities to any reform.

The correct answer is B.

Question 10 -Solution

This is a reasoning question.

We have been asked to draw a conclusion from the final sentence of the passage: "*In old days, the postmaster was often the station doctor, or some subaltern who had plenty of spare time on his hands; in the present day village schoolmasters are found in the remotest districts acting in the same capacity*".

This sentence follows after a quote by a historian praising Dalhousie's postal reform. Thus, the sentence implies that, after Dalhousie's postal reform, postmasters had no time to be doctors, as they used to be earlier when they had a lot of spare time (when the postal system was in disuse). However, now they are kept busy since the postal reforms. Now village schoolmasters perform that function, implying that they have a lot of free time to spare.

Let's analyze the options one by one.

(A) This option is **incorrect** because no such thing has been suggested at all in the passage.

(B) This option is **incorrect** because this is not true since the postal reforms were put into place; this may have been true before the reforms.

(C) This option is **correct** because this matches our deductions above.

(D) This option is **incorrect** because doctors' inclinations have not been discussed in the passage; thus, we cannot say that this is necessarily true.

The correct answer is C.

Question 11 -Solution

This is a tone question.

We have been asked to identify the author's tone towards Lord Dalhousie's work. The author seems highly appreciative of the work done by Lord Dalhousie, evidenced by his use of words such as "special contribution" (in the final sentence of the second paragraph), "most importantly" (in the third paragraph), "proof of success" (in the final paragraph) and by his presentation of a quote highlighting the importance of Dalhousie's work, among other things. All in all, the author seems to admire Lord Dalhousie's reform work.

Let's analyze the options one by one.

(A) This option is **incorrect** because "qualified approval" means "limited/restricted approval" but the author approves of Dalhousie's work wholeheartedly.

(B) This option is **correct** because this matches our deductions above. "Keen esteem" means "deep appreciation".

(C) This option is **incorrect** because "veiled reproof" means "hidden criticism" but the author has a distinctly positive tone towards Lord Dalhousie's work.

(D) This option is **incorrect** because the author does not have any skepticism (doubt) towards Lord Dalhousie's work, not disguised or direct.

The correct answer is B.

7.7   Passage 7 (The sustainability of Homo sapiens)

Understanding the Passage

This is a long passage of high difficulty level on the topic of anthropology.

Biomass is an ecological concept, and is defined as the total mass of all living organisms in a unit area or ecosystem at any given time.

Biomass is the total mass of all living members of a species. Considering all the species, human beings are one of the largest biomasses on earth [*Insects have the most biomass*]. They are the leading influence on earth's ecosystems, and, as a result of ecological processes, they inhabit most areas throughout the world. A species has a great chance of survival if its aggregate biomass is at the top when compared with other species. Since the biomass of human beings is at the top, they can claim their territory *(habitats)*, and take control of resources. [*For a species to survive, it must compete with other species and have influence, thereby leveraging sustainable resources*]It might be short-sighted to belittle the success of an emerging species or breed for being small in number if it is evident that the members of the species are well-adjusted [*The author says that while the aggregate biomass is one of the determinants of the species' success, it is not wise to think less of species with less biomass if they have good adaptations that allow them to adjust well with the environment*]. A species' ability to adapt to their habitat in the ecosystem, yet being varied according to the needs of the environment, is considered highly. Human beings have had nearly unparalleled success compared to other species in successful adaptation. As a result, human beings exist in huge numbers. It is a fact that human beings have remained in a generally undifferentiated form that allows them to rank highly as a single successful species. [*Human beings did not branch out in many different sub-species; they adapted themselves well and remained Homo sapiens. Usually when a species changes its habitat, or the environment around it changes, the species is forced to adapt to the new surroundings and often adapts and changes so much that it is no longer like the earlier species, and becomes a new variant.*]

Compared to other species, human beings are considered unique, as they retain their form as they travel from environment to environment. [*Other species, if adapted successfully, may lose their form.*] Despite challenges in the environment and adapting to new environments, human beings have been able to adjust their behavior sufficiently to avoid having nature make such extensive piecemeal adjustments to them that entirely distinct workable alternatives of the same model occupy the new space. [*It means that humans withstood nature's default adjustment of splitting a species into similar yet different variants of surviving species.*] And with these adjustments, other species such as dinosaurs transmogrified to pigeons, primitive fish to amphibians and then eventually to whales, even Homo sapiens *(human beings)* partially to Neanderthals (a similar yet different species of human) for a time. [*All these are examples of when nature stepped in to help any species to adapt to survive better and the final result was drastically different from the original form.*]

Typically, when ecological processes happen (rivers changing course, tectonic plates shifting or cracking, the emergence of mountain ranges, canyon formation, glacial melting or forming, the formation or destruction of land bridges, or the increase/decrease of large bodies of water), species get split and separated geographically. This fragmentation of species can permanently cause splits in the population, each fragment now subjected to different climatic and environmental challenges. To adapt to these changing situations, the genes change (drift apart), creating pools of differing genes within the population. This process can lead to the formation of totally different species from the separated species, and populations that can no longer mate with each other.

Surviving and altered variants of each species had to co-exist alongside their parental species [*Original species and newly-adapted and developed species live side-by-side*]. Many surviving species, with successful reproduction with other members, move into another ecosystem. Following this, each variant species was considered a different species, something other than its parent species [*Each variant becomes nearly completely different from the original ones —and probably can no longer mate with the original species*]. In this way, the exchange of genes among members occurred across the globe, and new species take on scientifically unique identities at different times and in different places. But humans remain a distinct species [*compared to other species, humans did not branch out to many variant species*] not because they are the first to exist in so many habitats and take advantage of so many resources, but because they have become one of the relatively few species to inhabitat different parts of the world in great numbers while being able to exchange genetic material [*sexual reproduction*] with others from their group, even if they had been largely geographically isolated from other groups over many generations. [*Humans are different because while they populated different habitats all over the world, unlike other species; they did not undergo such drastic changes that they could not continue to mate with other human beings from different parts. So, human beings are one of the most successful species ever.*] Thus, human beings are so marvelously successful as a species because, despite separation, evolution did not result in changes drastic enough to reproductively isolate separated humans.

Main Point: The survival and dominance of the species Homo Sapien.

Question 1-Solution

This is a detail question.

Option C is the correct answer, supported by the sentences given in the first part of paragraph 1: *"It can be said the most rudimentary measure of the **success of the species** is its position near the top of the aggregate biomass scale... For human beings, it is a reflection of **their claim on territory, and their consumption of resources as a species.**"*

Option A is classic case of mixing up words. The passage states *"It can be said the most rudimentary measure of the success of the species is **its position near the top of the aggregate biomass scale**, and not at the top of the food chain.*

Other options are either not stated in the passage or are inconclusive.

The correct answer is C.

Question 2-Solution

This is a detail question.

(A)   This option is **incorrect** because though the passage mentions that even Homo sapiens partially yielded to Neanderthals for a time through piecemeal adjustments, it does not make human beings unique in their colonization of the Earth. What makes human colonization unique, and unlike that of other species, is that while spreading to different habitats they did not adapt to the extent of becoming different from the original species. Most species change and adapt so much when they move to new habitats that they no longer resemble the original species.

(B)   This is the **correct** answer. It is supported by: *"Humans thus remain distinct (unique) not because they are the first to exist in so many habitats, and take advantage of so many resources, but in that they have become one of the relatively few organisms to accomplish widespread population of different habitats while being able to exchange genetic material with others from their group, even if they had been largely geographically isolated over many generations."* This implies that unlike other species, humans could avoid splitting into different species yet were able to habituate themselves densely in diversified habitats. Thus, they survived as one species even through their dispersal all over the world, and did not get differentiated and fragmented into different sub-species.

(C)   This option is **incorrect** because though it is correct that human beings are one of the highest ranked organisms on the biomass scale, it does not make human beings unique with respect to the colonization aspect. Also, insects are ranked higher than human beings on the biomass scale.

(D)   This option is **incorrect** because this is opposite of the fact given in the passage. Refer to the last part of the last paragraph; the gist is: "Humans thus remain distinct (unique)... because... they accomplish widespread population of different habitats while being able to exchange genetic material with others from their group, even if they had been largely geographically isolated over many generations.; it implies that human beings did not carry their genetic code to all parts of the world, yet succeeded in their colonization of the Earth."

The correct answer is B.

Question 3 -Solution

This is a detail question.

Option C is the correct answer. Since human beings had the ability to adjust themselves according to their environment, they could avoid the genetic splitting into different species. It is supported by: *"Still, human beings have been able to adjust their behavior sufficiently to avoid having nature make such extensive piecemeal adjustments to them that entirely distinct workable alternatives of the same model occupy the new space."* It means that humans escaped nature's default adjustment of splitting a species into similar yet different variants of surviving species by adjusting their behavior to suit the environment in which they were put.

Other options are either not stated in the passage or are not supported.

The correct answer is C.

Question 4-Solution

This is a detail question.

(A)   This option is **incorrect** because it is also not mentioned in the passage. How densely any species is populated is not mentioned.

(B)   This is the **correct** answer since the passage notes that it is the *"widespread population of different habitats (population size) while being able to exchange genetic material with others from their group"* which the passage notes as 'distinct' in terms of success over other species. That is how biomass is defined and success of a species is how much biomass it has accumulated.

(C)   This option is **incorrect** because the passage mentions that genetic code is dispersed around the world for any given species, but it is the ability of that species to retain its genetic code which is one of the criteria for success, and not merely the global dispersion of its genetic code.

(D)   This option is **incorrect** because as shown by the sentences *"It might be short-sighted to belittle the success of an emerging species or breed for being small in number if it is evident that the members of the species are elegant and well-adjusted. However, the ability to adapt one's habitat to the largest ecosystem, while still **retaining the flexibility to deal with local demands on the population may be considered high art in the annals of successful adaptation.**"* There are two factors to be taken into account for success, one: ability to adapt, and two: being flexible to deal with local demands of the population. Thus, the degree of adaptation to its environment by itself cannot be quantified as success.

The correct answer is B.

Question 5-Solution

This is a detail question.

The passage measures success in many parameters: species biomass (insects at the top, and humans near the top), capability to claim territory and consume resources, and adaptation to different environments. Option A is the correct answer since the passage discusses the effect of ecological change driving species into different habitats, which is related to geographic dispersion.

Other options are either not mentioned or are not inferable from the passage.

The correct answer is A.

Question 6-Solution

This is a function question.

Option D is the correct answer because the passage discusses the movement of human genetic material as human beings migrated across the earth. Refer to the last part of the last paragraph; the gist is: *"Humans thus remain distinct (unique)... because...they accomplish widespread population of different habitats while being able to **exchange genetic material (or,** _**migration of species**) with others from their group, even if they had been largely geograph-ically isolated over many generations._"

Other options are either not mentioned or are not inferable from the passage.

The correct answer is D.

Question 7-Solution

This is a detail question.

Option C is the correct answer since the passage is a detailed, fact-driven, objective, and impartial discussion of a topic. It is neither biased nor critical of the facts presented in the passage. It isn't vague or harshly critical (polemical) either. Thus, it can be best expressed as balanced.

The correct answer is C.

Question 8-Solution

This is a detail question.

We have been asked to provide evidence to explain the success of human beings on earth. Almost every paragraph discusses that the reason human beings are so successful is that they have spread across the globe, living in strikingly different ecosystems, but have not become reproductively isolated or become a new species.

Let's analyze the options one by one.

(A)   This option is **incorrect** because the sentence "_Biomass, in ecology, is the mass of living biological organisms in a given area or ecosystem at a given time_" does not discuss the success of human beings in particular, but provides a generic definition.

(B)   This option is **incorrect** because while the sentence "_However, the ability to adapt one's habitat to the largest ecosystem, while still retaining the flexibility to deal with local demands on the population may be considered high art in the annals of successful adaptation_" contains discussions of the success of some species in general, it does not discuss the success of human beings in particular.

(C)   This option is **correct** because the sentence "_Thus, human beings are so successful as a species because despite separation, evolution did not result in changes drastic enough to reproductively isolate separated humans_" matches our deductions above.

(D)   This option is **incorrect** because the sentence "_As a result, human beings exist in huge numbers_" only discusses human beings, but not the reason for their success.

The correct answer is C.

Question 9-Solution

This is a tone question.

We have to figure out the author's tone towards the success of human beings on earth. While generally the author seems removed from the discussion, in the final sentence, the author's use of the word "marvelously" shows that the author seems more positive than neutral towards the success of human beings.

Let's analyze the options one by one.

(A) This option is **incorrect** because while the author seems to be in support of human beings, we cannot choose "capricious endorsement" which means "changing/unpredictable approval", since the author does not seem to have changing views.

(B) This option is **incorrect** because the author is not negative towards the success of human beings. "Sharp disparagement" means "deep/cutting criticism/disapproval".

(C) This option is **incorrect** because even though the author seems mainly neutral, he eventually does express some positive judgment about the success of human beings, however slight.

(D) This option is **correct** because this matches our deductions above. "Tentative approbation" means "slight/unsure approval".

The correct answer is D.

Chart for questions # 10 & 11

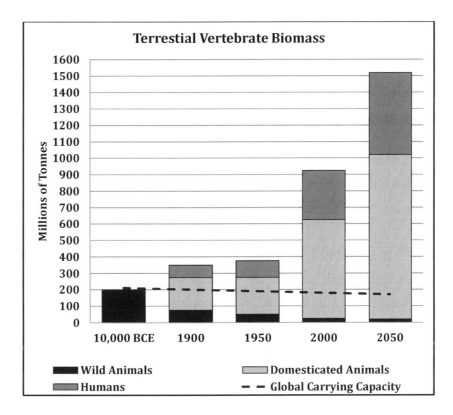

Question 10-Solution

We have to calculate the greatest percentage increase of the biomass of humans from one period to the next period.

Let us analyze each option on by one.

(A) 1900-1950: The biomass in the year 1900 was approximately 75, and in the year 1950 was approximately 100, thus the percentage increase = $\frac{100-75}{75} * 100\% = \frac{25}{75} * 100\% = 33.33\%$. There is no need to be very precise in reading the data values; do your best as per your ability. The data in the graph are such that a considerable error in reading will not change the answer.

(B) 1950-2000: We know that the biomass in the year 1950 was approximately 100, and in the year 2000 was approximately 300, thus the percentage increase = $\frac{300-100}{100} * 100\% = \frac{200}{100} * 100\% = 200\%$.

(C) 2000-2050: We know that the biomass in the year 2000 was approximately 300, and in the year 2050 was approximately 500, thus the percentage increase = $\frac{500-300}{300} * 100\% = \frac{200}{300} * 100\% = 66.67\%$.

Since 200% is the greatest increase, clearly the correct answer is option B.

The correct answer is B.

Question 11-Solution

The question wants us to deduce the trends of the biomasses of three species: wild animals, domesticated animals, and humans.

From the chart, we find that the biomass of wild animals has been continuously decreasing from the period 10,000 BCE to 2050, and that of domesticated animals and that of humans have been continuously increasing, though marginally, from the period of 1900-1950. Thus the correct answer is option C.

The correct answer is C.

7.8   Passage 8 (The influence of the British poetry of World War One)

Understanding the Passage

This is a long passage of higher difficultly level on a critical commentary on historical literature.

Perhaps the most persistent myth about British poetry of World War One is that it became progressively more realistic as soldier-poets learned more about the horrors of modern trench warfare. *{There is a stubborn myth. The myth is that British poetry during WWI became more and more realistic as soldiers who were the poets got deeper and deeper into a modern type of warfare known as trench warfare.}* According to this orthodoxy, the `pastoral` patriotism of Brooke soon gave way, in the mud and blood of Flanders, to the angry realism of Sassoon and Owen. *{According to this orthodox belief, calm and serene patriotic poems like those written by Brooke decreased, and angry, realistic poems, possibly depicting the muddy, bloody situation in Flanders (a place), like those written by Sassoon and Owen increased.}* Thus when we think of World War One poetry today, the poems that instantly come to the minds of most readers are those angry and satirical anti-war poems, such as Sassoon's "Base Details" and "Blighters" ,and Owen's "Dulce et decorum est," the last being probably the most famous, certainly the most widely anthologized, poem of the war. *{This is why when we think about WWI poetry, the angry, sarcastic poems written by Sassoon and Owen come to mind. Owen's "Dulce et decorum est," is possibly the most famous and most widely anthologized (published) poem of that time.}* The problem with this view is that it is based on a relatively small group of poems that, despite their indisputable excellence, are in many ways atypical of the bulk of poetry, including much of the good poetry, written during the war. *{There is a problem with this myth/view. The problem is that such angry poems were written, but these angry poems represent a minor proportion of WWI poetry. The bulk of WWI poetry, which includes most of the good poetry from that time, is not typically angry or sarcastic.}* `That poetry` was deeply indebted to the nineteenth-century poetic tradition running from Wordsworth and the Romantics through the major Victorian poets to Hardy and beyond. *{Most of that poetry is inspired by the 19th century poetic style from Wordsworth (of the Romantic style) to Hardy (of the Victorian style). Thus, the bulk of WWI poetry was written in the 19th century Romantic and Victorian styles.}* The majority of the war poets worked within this tradition to produce, as has been recently argued, the trench lyric. *{Most of the war's soldier-poets worked in this 19th century Romantic and Victorian style and created a new style called the trench lyric (the new style was called "trench" because the soldiers were conducting the "trench" style of warfare, some form of modern warfare.)}* But it is not just much of the poetry of World War One that belongs to this tradition. *{However, it is not only WWI poetry which was made in this 19th century Romantic and Victorian style. Some WWI prose, too, followed this style.}* The last two paragraphs of what many regard as one of the best memoirs to come out of the war, Siegfried Sassoon's "Memoirs of a Fox-Hunting Man" (1928), emerge from the same tradition and constitute a prose version of the trench lyric composed by the solider-poets. *{The last two paragraphs of Sassoon's memoirs also follow the 19th century Romantic and Victorian style. This book is considered to be among the best memoirs of WWI.}*

At first glance, a work by the author of some of the bitterest and most angry anti-war poems of World War One may seem an unlikely place to observe the conventions (rules and methodology) of Romantic poetry, but the ending of "Memoirs of a Fox-Hunting Man" reveals just how insistently the Romantic lyric imposed its form and structure on the imaginations of the writers of World War One. *{Initially, it may seem impossible that a bitter and angry anti-war poem might contain the 19th century Romantic and Victorian style; however, the ending of that memoir demonstrates that the 19th century Romantic and Victorian style was very deeply embedded in the minds of WWI poets and writers.}* Readers have consistently noted how the language of the last two paragraphs of "Memoirs of a Fox-Hunting Man" self-consciously echoes Thomas Hardy's "The Darkling Thrush." *{Readers have always noted similarities between last two paragraphs of Sassoon's memoirs and Hardy's poems.}* But it is not just a single poem by Hardy that lies behind the end of Memoirs of a Fox-Hunting Man. *{However, the similarities are not limited to just that.}* Sassoon is doing more than including an oblique reference to a specific poem. *{It seems like Sassoon has referenced Hardy's work purposely.}* Both Hardy's lyric and the ending of Sassoon's fictional memoir belong to a structurally identifiable Romantic and Victorian lyric genre running from early Wordsworth and Coleridge to such late nineteenth-century incarnations as Hardy's lyric and on into the twentieth century. *{Both works are similar because they belong to the same tradition in writing.}* By imitating this form of the Romantic and post-Romantic lyric, Sassoon is aligning himself with a tradition of English poetry and a particular lyric form more than a century old. *{Sassoon is showing support for the tradition by referencing Hardy's poem.}* So strongly had this genre enforced itself upon the literary consciousness of poets and readers alike that, by the end of the nineteenth century, it had become virtually synonymous with the lyric poem. *{This genre is very deeply embedded in the psyche of poets, too deeply to be changed or removed.}* The soldier-poets of the Great War carried this model with them in their minds and in their copies of The Oxford Book of English Verse into the trenches of France and Flanders, along with their rifles, their kitbags, and (before long) their gas masks. *{The soldier-poets, knowingly or unknowingly, stuck to this tradition, in any work that they created.}*

Sassoon, like Rosenberg, does not abandon a set of worn-out poetic conventions so he can write directly and realistically, and hence originally, about it. Rather he translates a pre-existing model into local terms. *{Both Sassoon and Rosenberg write realistically using the same poetic conventions. They do not ditch conventions completely. Instead, Sassoon uses the existing convention and customizes it to his need.}* Even literary memoirists, who are expected to respect the facts, can only be as realistic as the artificial literary conventions available to them will allow them to be. *{Even professional memoirists use existing conventions, and so soldier poets would, too (Memoirs — a style of biography; memoirists — biographers).}* Writers write realistically not by directly "telling it like it is," but by telling it like it's told in literature. *{Writers are realistic not by writing reality but by writing conventionally about reality.}* They must, as Northrop Frye told us half a century ago, find, or adapt, a set of literary conventions, and out of this old paradigm create a new literary form. *{Writers adapt conventions to make new forms}*, and he famously states "Poetry is made out of other poems." {Frye believes that all poetry is created from earlier poetry.}

Main Point: British poetry did not become more and more realistic during WWI; the trench lyric was formed by adapting an existing style, not by creating a new one.

Question 1-Solution

This is a main Purpose question from the general category.

The question asks us to choose the primary purpose of the passage.

The author first presents a myth about British poetry of the war and then explains why she believes that the myth is incorrect. She provides examples to make her point and ends the passage with a generalized idea of what the war poetry actually is. Thus, she wishes to debunk the myth that war poetry became more and more realistic when soldiers who were poets learned about modern warfare, and disprove the theory that earlier poetic convention was replaced by a new one.

Let's analyze the options one by one.

(A)   This is the **correct** answer. This can be accurately described as the primary purpose.

(B)   This option is **incorrect** because the author's intention isn't just to discuss British war poetry, but to negate a particular myth about it.

(C)   This option is **incorrect** because the author discusses nineteenth century Romantic and Victorian poets only as a basis for war poetry, and not as a point in itself.

(D)   This option is **incorrect** because the author implies the opposite of this option. The author suggests that new styles are created by adapting existing styles, and not by themselves.

The correct answer is A.

Question 2-Solution

This is a detail question.

The question asks us to choose an option with which the author will agree.

Let's analyze the options one by one.

(A)   This is **incorrect** because the author mentions that Owen's "Dulce et decorum est" is the most famous poem of the war and uses it as an example of poetry that is not characteristic or representative of the bulk of war poetry. Thus, the author will not agree with this statement.

(B)   This is the **correct** option because the bulk of poetry (referred to as "that poetry") is influenced by nineteenth-century poetic tradition, which is defined by Wordsworth and the Romantics and also the major Victorian poets. The majority of war poets worked within this nineteenth-century tradition to produce the trench lyric. Thus, the author will agree with this statement

(C)   This is **incorrect** because this is against the main point of the author. The author implies that new styles are created by adapting existing styles, and not by themselves, and specifically that the famous war poetry is derived from the nineteenth-century tradition. Thus, the author will not agree with this statement.

(D)   This option is **incorrect** because the author does not discuss Sassoon as a main point. Sassoon is mentioned as an example.

The correct answer is B.

Question 3-Solution

This is an inference question.

We have been asked to choose an option that states the author's reason for believing that World War One poetry did not become more realistic and evolve into a different literary form.

Let's analyze the options one by one.

(A)   This is the **correct** option because the passage states that the bulk of poetry (referred to as "that poetry", and highlighted in the passage) is influenced by nineteenth-century poetic tradition, which is defined by Wordsworth and the Romantics and also the major Victorian poets. The majority of war poets worked within this nineteenth-century tradition to produce the trench lyric.

(B)   This option is **incorrect** because the author believes the opposite of this option. The author suggests that new styles are created by adapting existing styles, and not by themselves. Thus, she wouldn't agree that pastoral patriotism gave way to the angry realism of war poets, which led to the formation of the trench lyric.

(C)   This is **incorrect** because the opposite of this is suggested by the author in the last part of the passage. It states that Sassoon did not give up completely the poetic conventions of the nineteenth-century poetic tradition, but that he adapted them according to circumstances and the time. This adaptation is the "realistic" version of earlier conventions, and not an original invention. The last part also states that writers adapt or develop supposedly new forms from old conventions.

(D)   This is **incorrect** because we cannot necessarily infer that the author believes what she believes because Frye mentions something. Such a connection has not been suggested in the passage.

The correct answer is A.

Question 4 -Solution

This is an inference question.

The answer to this question lies in the highlighted sentences (reproduced here) — "Thus when we think of World War One poetry ... much of the poetry of World War One that belongs to this tradition." In this part of the passage, the author explains that most people tend to think of World War poetry as angry and satirical anti-war poems, but those angry poems are **atypical (i.e. not representative)** of the bulk of War poetry. Then the author uses the term that poetry, and states that "that poetry" owes a debt to nineteenth century poetry, the style on which the majority of war poetry is based. Thus "that poetry" refers to the "bulk of war poetry" but not to the "angry poetry", which is different from the bulk of war poetry. Also, we cannot say that the term "that poetry" can refer to all poetry from the World War because then it would include the "angry poetry".

Thus, the correct answer is D.

Question 5-Solution

This is a function question.

We have been asked to find an alternative to the word ▐pastoral▐ , as used in the passage.

Let's analyze the sentence: "the **pastoral patriotism** of Brooke soon gave way ... to the **angry realism** of Sassoon and Owen". Thus, "pastoral patriotism" was replaced by "angry realism". So, "pastoral" is relatively contradictory to "angry".

Let's analyze the options one by one.

(A)   This is the **correct** answer. This can very well serve as a replacement for "pastoral" because it is contextually contradictory to "angry". "Serene" means "calm, undisturbed".

(B)   This option is **incorrect** because it is not contextually contradictory to "angry realism".

(C)   This option is **incorrect** because "divine — holy, godly" is out of context of the passage and the sentence.

(D)   This option is **incorrect** because "satirical — sarcastic" is a negative word; "pastoral" is contextually positive.

The correct answer is A.

Question 6 -Solution

This is a detail question.

We have been asked to choose a sentence in which the author **demonstrates** that Sassoon's work "Memoirs of a Fox-Hunting Man" is in keeping with the nineteenth century poetic tradition of the Romantic and Victorian poets.

While Sassoon's work "Memoirs of a Fox-Hunting Man" is first mentioned in the previous sentence: "The last two paragraphs of what many ... composed by the solider-poets"; the author proves that it follows the nineteenth century poetic tradition in "At first glance, a work by the ... the writers of World War One", especially in the part "... the ending of "Memoirs of a Fox-Hunting Man" reveals just how insistently the Romantic lyric imposed its form and structure ...".

The sentence (option A) "Sassoon, like Rosenberg, does not ... and hence originally, about it" merely discusses connections between Sassoon's work and the trench lyric but not to the poetic tradition of the Romantic and Victorian poets. Option D is too generic and not specific to Sassoon's work "Memoirs of a Fox-Hunting Man".

Thus, only the sentence (option C) "At first glance, a work by the ... the writers of World War One" **demonstrates** that Sassoon's work "Memoirs of a Fox-Hunting Man" is in keeping with the nineteenth century poetic tradition of the Romantic and Victorian poets.

The correct answer is C.

Question 7 -Solution

This is a tone question.

We have been asked to describe the author's attitude towards the view that increasingly modern warfare rendered the poetry of the war more and more angry and sarcastic. This view is discussed by the author in the first sentence of the passage. The author calls this view "the most persistent myth". Thus, it is clear that the author does not believe in this view. However, we cannot say that she fully disagrees with this view because she states that this myth is persistent, as it is based on some (famous) poems that do not reflect the bulk of war poetry. Thus, she believes that the myth holds true for some of the poems but not for most of the poems or prose. Thus, her attitude towards the myth can be thought of as partial disagreement.

Let's analyze the options one by one.

(A) This option is **incorrect**. Qualified enthusiasm — Limited enthusiasm; using "enthusiasm", even if "limited", for partial disagreement is one step too far from the actual attitude.

(B) This option is **incorrect**. Utter disgust; the author does not bear disgust towards the myth. The author is quite objective; she logically disagrees with it and does not let emotions color her judgment.

(C) This option is **incorrect**. Healthy regard; this does not express any of her partial disagreement of the myth.

(D) This option is **correct**. Cautious dubiety — Controlled skepticism/doubt; this expresses the author's partial disagreement in the best way; the author is skeptical of believing the persistent myth.

The correct answer is D.

Question 8 -Solution

This is a reasoning question.

We have been asked to draw a conclusion from the final quote made by Northrop Frye: "Poetry is made out of other poems." From this, we can deduce that Frye believes that any poem is dependent on earlier poetry, in keeping with his ideas about writers adapting conventions instead of creating new ones.

Let's analyze the options one by one.

(A) This option is **incorrect** because this is the opposite of what can be concluded from the final quote made by Northrop Frye.

(B) This option is **incorrect** because Frye's final quote does not specifically apply to Sassoon; it is more general. Also, this option is too extreme.

(C)   This option is **correct** because this matches our deductions above.

(D)   This option is **incorrect** because this option is too extreme. Frye suggests that every poem is based on earlier poetry, but not that no idea can be at all new.

The correct answer is C.

Question 9 -Solution

We have been asked to find a sentence which provides the answer for why solider-poets wrote trench lyrics in the nineteenth-century poetic tradition. Thus, it must be a generic sentence, explaining why solider-poets were influenced by the nineteenth-century poetic tradition.

Let's analyze the options one by one.

(A)   This option is **incorrect** because the sentence *"Readers have consistently noted how the language of the last two paragraphs of "Memoirs of a Fox-Hunting Man" self-consciously echoes Thomas Hardy's "The Darkling Thrush""* is particular to Sassoon and does not explain in general why solider-poets were influenced by the nineteenth-century poetic tradition.

(B)   This option is **correct** because the sentence *"So strongly had this genre enforced itself upon the literary consciousness of poets and readers alike that, by the end of the nineteenth century, it had become virtually synonymous with the lyric poem"* explains why solider-poets were influenced by the poetic tradition and is not particular to any poet.

(C)   This option is **incorrect** because the sentence *"Both Hardy's lyric and the ending of Sassoon's fictional memoir belong to a structurally identifiable Romantic and Victorian lyric genre running from the early Wordsworth and Coleridge to such late nineteenth-century incarnations as Hardy's lyric and on into the twentieth century"* is particular to Hardy and Sassoon and does not explain in general why solider-poets were influenced by the nineteenth-century poetic tradition.

(D)   This option is **incorrect** because the sentence *"Sassoon is doing more than including an oblique reference to a specific poem"* is particular to Sassoon and does not explain in general why solider-poets were influenced by the poetic tradition.

The correct answer is B.

Question 10 -Solution

We have been asked to choose a poet whose poetry is similar in tone to Sassoon's **poetry**. We know from the first paragraph that Sassoon's poetry is angry and satirical, similar to Owen's. However, his prose (Memoirs …) is similar to Hardy's poem. Brooke's style is pastoral patriotism, which was replaced by Sassoon's and Owen's. Thus Sassoon cannot be similar to Brooke in the tone of his poetry. Frye's poems have not been discussed at all to compare with Sassoon's.

Thus, the only inferable similarity is between the tones of the poetry of Sassoon and Owen.

The correct answer is B.

Question 11 -Solution

This is a parallel reasoning question.

We have been asked to find a scenario most similar to the situation of Sassoon's writing. We know that Sassoon does not create a new system, but adapts a current one. Thus, we need to find a scenario in which something is made from an existing thing, and not created originally.

Let's analyze the options one by one.

(A)   This option is **correct** because in this scenario, something is created by adapting an existing thing, much like Sassoon did.

(B)   This option is **incorrect** because in this scenario, we do not know whether the new product line was created by adapting an existing line or in a completely original way.

(C)   This option is **incorrect** because in this scenario something is created in a completely original way, not by adapting an existing thing. Thus, this is the opposite of what Sassoon did.

(D)   This option is **incorrect** because in this scenario, we do not know whether the song was created by adapting an existing song/melody or in a completely original way.

The correct answer is A.

7.9 Passage 9 (New evidence clears up a long puzzle)

Understanding the passage

This is a medium length passage of high difficulty level on life sciences.

The earliest accumulation of oxygen in the atmosphere is arguably the most important biological event in Earth's history. *{An increase in concentration of oxygen is an important event, because the development of animal life depends on it.}* A general consensus asserts that appreciable oxygen first accumulated in Earth's atmosphere around 2.3 billion years ago during the so-called Great Oxidation Event (GOE). *{Scientists generally agree that an adequate amount of oxygen accumulated in the atmosphere around 2.3 billion years ago, in an event called GOE.}* Scientists have long speculated as to why animal species didn't burgeon sooner, once sufficient oxygen covered the Earth's surface. *{Scientists have been unable to fully understand why animals did not thrive sooner, at the time when oxygen was adequate even though plants had long started appearing and developing.}* Animals first appeared and began to prosper at the end of the Proterozoic period, about 600 to 700 million years ago—but the billion-year stretch before that, when there was also plenty of oxygen, there were no animals. *{Oxygen was sufficient for about a billion years before animals actually appeared. Animals appeared at the end of the Proterozoic period, about 600 to 700 million years ago, but there was plenty of oxygen for about a billion years before that.}*

Evidently, the air was not oxygen-rich enough then. The oxygen levels during the billion or more years before the rise of animals were only 0.1 percent of what they are today. *{The answer to this puzzle is that it seemed like there was enough oxygen, but actually there was not. Oxygen was only 0.1% of today's level.}* In other words, Earth's atmosphere couldn't have supported a diversity of creatures, no matter what genetic advancements were in place. *{So, oxygen is necessary for the development of animals, and without it, the development of animals is simply not possible.}* While there is no question that genetic and ecological innovations are ultimately behind the rise of animals, there is also no question that for animal life to flourish a certain level of oxygen is required. *{Thus, earlier oxygen estimates were incorrect. Based on the old, incorrect oxygen estimates, scientists wondered how much oxygen is necessary. However, the latest data proves that a higher amount of oxygen is necessary, just as genetic and ecological adaptations are required for animals to flourish.}* The evidence was found by analyzing chromium isotopes in ancient sediments from China, Australia, Canada, and the United States. *{This new evidence of required oxygen levels was found by analyzing chromium isotopes from four countries.}* Chromium is found in the Earth's continental crust, and chromium oxidation, the process recorded by the chromium isotopes, is directly linked to the presence of free oxygen in the atmosphere. *{Chromium isotopes are used because they are directly proportional to the amount of free oxygen. So, analyzing chromium isotopes can give a clue about the oxygen levels of the atmosphere. Chromium isotopes are created by oxidation; they are present in the Earth's crust.}* Specifically, samples deposited in shallow, iron-rich ocean areas were studied, near the ancient shoreline and compared with other samples taken from younger shoreline locales deposited in similar settings but known to have higher levels of oxygen. *{To get specific details, chromium isotopes from both old and new crusts were collected to get an idea of how much oxygen was present in the past and how much is now.}*

The question about the role of oxygen in controlling the first appearance of animals has long vexed scientists. *{Scientists have long searched for the answer to the question of the connection between oxygen level and when the first animals came into being .}* Previous estimates, which put the oxygen level at 40 percent of today's conditions during pre-animal times, were based on very loose constraints, leaving open the possibility that oxygen was already plenty high to support animal life, and shifting the absence of animal life before the end of the Proterozoic to other controls. *{Earlier estimates of oxygen levels, before chromium data, were based on loose constraints. This led to the estimate that the oxygen level was 40% of today's level, but it actually was only 0.1%. Since oxygen was thought to be sufficient, scientists began to think that the later appearance of animals must be linked to some other factor, and not oxygen.}* Oxygen levels were highly dynamic in the early atmosphere, with the potential for occasional spikes. *{Oxygen levels were very changeable in the early days, and occasionally rose sharply, too.}* However, it also seems clear that there are first-order differences in the nature of the Earth's surface chromium cycling before the rise of animals versus the time interval coincident with their first appearance, implying extremely low oxygen conditions before. *{However, it is clear that oxygen was in very small amounts, not enough to support animal appearance or rise. Chromium cycling changed around the time of the appearance of animals, proving that the earlier oxygen level was insufficient.}* These differences are recorded in a dramatic shift in the chromium isotope data, with clear signals of cycling beneath a more oxygen-rich atmosphere at the time the animals appear. *{The differences in the chromium cycling data proves that oxygen became plentiful around the time the animals appeared.}*

The late Proterozoic—the time period beginning less than a billion years ago following this remarkable chapter of sustained low levels of oxygen—was strikingly different, marked by extreme climatic events manifested in global-scale glaciation, indications of at least intervals of modern-like oxygen abundances, and the emergence and diversification of the earliest animals. *{The time period that began a little less than a billion years ago is known as the late Proterozoic period. In this period, oxygen levels were low and there were extreme climatic events such as glacier formation, short bursts of adequate oxygen levels, and the development of the earliest animals.}* Oxygen played a major if not dominant role in the timing of that rise and, in particular, in the subsequent emergence of complex ecologies for animal life on and within the sediment, predator-prey relationships, and large bodies. *{Oxygen had an important part to play in the rise of animals, their sustaining ecologies, and the like.}*

Main point: New evidence solves a long-standing puzzle about the relevance of oxygen in the appearance of animals.

Question 1-Solution

This is an inference question.

We have to choose an option that provides the most accurate inference implied by the new evidence. The answer to this question lies in the final paragraph, which states that previous estimates were based on very loose constraints, leaving open the possibility that oxygen was already plenty high to support animal life, and shifting the absence of animal life before the end of the Proterozoic to other factors. Thus, the earlier estimates were incorrect, making the scientists feel that animals could have existed before end of the Proterozoic period. However, new evidence shows that oxygen levels were so dynamic and low that animals could not have existed then.

Let's analyze the options one by one.

(A)   This option is **incorrect** because the passage proves the opposite of this – that animals could not have existed then.

(B)   This option is **incorrect** because the passage proves the opposite of this – that oxygen levels were dynamic and low before end of the Proterozoic period.

(C)   This option is **incorrect** because the passage does not set out to prove the existence of chromium cycles. This is not an inference, but a stated fact.

(D)   This is the **correct** option. It matches our deductions. The passage proves that oxygen levels were dynamic and low before the end of the Proterozoic period, and that the earlier estimates were incorrect.

The correct answer is D.

Question 2-Solution

This is a reasoning question on weakening the conclusion.

We have to choose an option that would weaken the claim made in the final paragraph.

The final paragraph states that previous estimates of oxygen were based on very loose constraints, leaving open the possibility that oxygen was plenty high to support animal life, and shifting the absence of animal life before the end of the Proterozoic to other factors. Thus, the earlier estimates were incorrect, making the scientists feel that animals could have existed before the end of the Proterozoic period. However, new evidence shows that oxygen levels were so dynamic and low that animals could not have existed then. Therefore, the claim being made in the final paragraph is that animals did not exist before the end of the Proterozoic period despite plenty of oxygen because, in fact, there was not plenty of oxygen. This claim is based on evidence in the second paragraph. Chromium oxidation cycles were studied from shoreline samples. We have to weaken the claim.

Let's analyze the options one by one.

(A)   This option is **incorrect** because stating that chromium oxidation is the only reliable indicator of oxygen levels strengthens the claim, which is based on those cycles.

(B)   This option is **incorrect** because stating that oxygen levels required to sustain animal life are far higher than currently believed strengthens the claim, which stated that oxygen levels were lower than thought. Thus, if the required oxygen level is higher than was thought, the lower than estimated oxygen could not have sustained animal life at all.

(C)   This option is **incorrect** because stating that chromium samples from other continents match the samples from Australia strengthens the claim, which is based on those levels.

(D)   This is the **correct** option because stating that shoreline locales are not quite representative of the rest of the landforms weakens the claim, which is based on chromium samples from shoreline locales. On the basis of samples from shorelines, claims about oxygen and animal life were made. However, if shoreline areas are not representative of the rest of the land, the claims will not apply to the rest of the land, leaving open the possibility that oxygen could have been high enough to sustain animal life, thus weakening the claim in the final paragraph.

The correct answer is D.

Question 3-Solution

This is a function question.

We have to choose an option that best describes the role of the second paragraph in the whole passage.

In the first paragraph, the author explains that a particular question has always bothered scientists - why animal species didn't flourish sooner, once sufficient oxygen covered the Earth's surface. The author explains the background for this question. In the second paragraph, the author presents some new evidence that begins to explain how the question can be answered. Thus, the second paragraph is providing evidence to answer the question presented in the first paragraph, to support the claim made in the last line of the first paragraph.

Let's analyze the options one by one.

(A)   This option is **incorrect** because the second paragraph presents new evidence, and does not elaborate on the things discussed in the first one.

(B)   This is the **correct** option. It matches our deductions. The second paragraph is buttressing (supporting) the first paragraph.

(C)   This option is **incorrect** because the second paragraph does not provide an alternative explanation. That is done by the third one.

(D)   This option is **incorrect** because the second paragraph does not offset (negate) the theory of the first one.

The correct answer is B.

Question 4 -Solution

This is a main purpose question from the general category.

The question asks us to find the primary purpose of the passage.

Let's analyze the passage.

The author first reveals that a particular question has always bothered the scientists - why animal species didn't flourish sooner, once sufficient oxygen covered the Earth's surface. The author explains the background for this question.

In the second paragraph, the author presents some new evidence that begins to explain how the question can be answered.

In the final paragraph, it becomes clear that the question itself is incorrect because it relied on incorrect data. Thus, the author is concerned with refuting an old belief ,or myth, and providing new evidence to dispel that belief.

Let's analyze the options one by one.

(A) This option is **incorrect** because the passage does not only discuss a scientific phenomenon, but also provides new evidence to dispel an old belief.

(B) This option is **incorrect** because the passage does not explain the origin of life, but discusses the origin of animals.

(C) This option is **incorrect** because the passage does not provide any hypothesis or support for it.

(D) This is the **correct** option. It matches our deductions.

The correct answer is D.

Question 5-Solution

This is an inference question.

We have been asked to choose an option that was believed to be true by scientists, that is, the statement that is no longer true, or has been disputed by the new evidence.

Let's analyze the options one by one.

(A) This is the **correct** option, as this must have been believed to be true by scientists earlier. The second sentence of the third paragraph (line # 24-25) states that previous estimates put the oxygen level at 40 percent of today's conditions during pre-animal times. However, these estimates have been disputed. The oxygen levels during the billion or more years before the rise of animals were only 0.1 percent of what they are today.

(B) This is an **incorrect** option because the fact that animals first appeared 600 to 700 million years ago was never called into question, and is still considered true.

(C) This is an **incorrect** option, as scientists must have believed the opposite of this. The scientists had an inflated estimate of oxygen. Scientists had long been puzzling over why animals had not appeared sooner, despite having plenty of oxygen. Thus, they must have believed that oxygen levels did not influence the appearance of animals.

(D) This is an **incorrect** option because the fact that for animal life to flourish a certain level of oxygen is required was never called into question, and is still considered true.

The correct answers is A.

Question 6 -Solution

This is a detail question.

We have to choose a statement that is still considered true.

Let's analyze the options one by one.

(A)   This option is **incorrect** because the opposite of this is stated in the final sentence of the first paragraph (line # 6-9) – that there is no question that for animal life to flourish a certain level of oxygen is required.

(B)   This option is also **incorrect** because the opposite of this is stated in the third sentence of the third paragraph (line # 30-31).

(C)   This option is **correct** because this is stated in the final sentence of the third paragraph (line # 34-36) – that there are clear signals of a more oxygen-rich atmosphere at the time the animals appear.

(D)   This option is also **incorrect** because the second sentence of the third paragraph (line # 26-28) states that previous estimates put the oxygen level at 40 percent of today's conditions during pre-animal times. However, these estimates have been disputed. The oxygen levels during the billion or more years before the rise of animals were only 0.1 percent of what they are today. Thus, the early levels were not high enough to support animals.

The correct answer is C.

Question 7 -Solution

This is a function question.

We have to find a replacement for the highlighted word burgeon as used in the context of the passage. The sentence is "Scientists have long speculated as to why animal species didn't bur-geon sooner, once sufficient oxygen covered the Earth's surface. Animals first **appeared** and began to **prosper** at the end of the Proterozoic period" So, animals appeared and prospered at the end of the Proterozoic period and scientists have wondered why they did not burgeon sooner. Thus, "burgeon" would be similar to "appear and prosper".

Let's look at the options one by one.

(A)   This is **correct** because "flourish" means "grow, thrive".

(B)   This is **incorrect** because "dwindle" means "decline in numbers".

(C)   This is **incorrect** because "wane" means "reduce".

(D)   This is **incorrect** because "evolve" does not necessarily mean "appear and prosper". It is closer in meaning to "change"; however, we need something similar to "thrive".

The correct answer is A.

Question 8 -Solution

This is a tone question.

We have been asked to find the tone of the scientists towards the Great Oxidation Event and the rise of animal species before the evidence from chromium data. The passage states, in the first paragraph, that scientists have long been puzzled as to why animal species did not de-velop sooner once oxygen was plentiful (as was believed before the evidence from chromium data). The final paragraph also mentions that this question "vexed" (annoyed and agitated) scientists. Thus, a word closest to "vexed" and "puzzled" would give us the right answer.

Let's analyze the options one by one.

(A)   This option is **correct** because this matches our deductions above. "Exasperated" means "vexed" and "annoyed".

(B)   This option is **incorrect** because "disgusted" is too strong a tone for "annoyed".

(C)   This option is **incorrect** because "cognizant" means "knowledgeable/in the know" and scientists were "puzzled" or "not in the know".

(D)   This option is **incorrect** because "elated" or "happy" is out of context.

The correct answer is A.

Question 9 -Solution

This is a function question from the general category.

We have to find the paragraph that **provides evidence** that clears up the long standing puzzle about the rise and development of animal species. Thus, we don't need just the claim, but also the evidence to explain why animal species did not evolve sooner.

The first paragraph explains the puzzle that scientists have been dealing with.

The second paragraph provides the answer to the puzzle – that the estimates of oxygen were believed to be much higher than they actually were. However, the second paragraph provides no evidence to back this claim.

The third paragraph **provides evidence** to back the claim made in the second paragraph.

The final paragraph merely sums everything up in a generic manner. So, clearly, the third paragraph is the correct answer.

The correct answer is C.

Charts for questions # 10 & 11

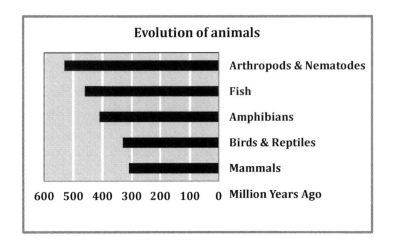

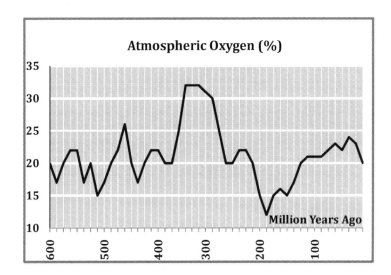

Question 10 -Solution

We have to deduce which of the following statements is supported by the passage and the graphs, taken together in consideration.

Let us analyze each option on by one.

(A)   This is **incorrect** because from the passage (Line # 38-39), we know that there was a low level of oxygen in the late Proterozoic period (a period 600 million years ago).

(B)   This is **incorrect** because from the passage (Line # 5), we know that plants (living organisms) had already evolved 600 million years ago.

(C)   This is **incorrect** because from the passage (Line # 30-31), we know that *oxygen levels were highly dynamic in the early atmosphere, with the potential for occasional spikes.* Thus we cannot conclusively deduce that, 600 million years ago, the oxygen level must have been less than 20% on Earth; it may have been more than 20% for a certain period, and then dropped sharply below 20%.

(D) This is **correct** because from the passage (Line # 11), we know that by the end of the Proterozoic period (about 600 to 700 million years ago), evidently, the air was not oxygen-rich enough.

The correct answer is D.

Question 11 -Solution

The question wants us to deduce the evolution of five categories of animals based on the percentage level of oxygen on the earth.

Let us analyze each option one by one.

(A) This is **incorrect** because from the chart, we find that the oxygen level reached 25% for the first time between 400-500 million years ago, but at that time only arthropods & nematodes and fish had evolved, so the statement is not supported.

(B) This is **correct** because from the chart, we find that the oxygen level reached its maximum level between 300 and 400 million years ago and remained that way until 300 million years ago, by which time mammals had evolved. So the statement that all five categories of animals had evolved once the oxygen level reached its maximum percentage level on the earth is supported.

(C) This is **incorrect** because from the chart, we find that the oxygen level reached 20% for the first time between 500-600 million years ago, but at that time only arthropods & nematodes had evolved, so the statement is not supported.

(D) This is **incorrect** because from the chart, we find that the oxygen level reached 25% for the second time between 300-400 million years ago, but at that time only arthropods & nematodes, amphibians, and fish had evolved, so the statement is not supported.

The correct answer is B.

7.10   Passage 10: Paired passage (BRICS economies)

Passage 1 (Mike, Chief Economist, on BRICS countries)

Understanding the Passage

The notion that the era of emerging BRICS countries is over, and that among them only China would make it to the group of high-income countries is outlandish. *{Mike believes that emerging BRICS countries are still going to be dominant at this time; their era is not over yet.}* No doubt the growth rates in the BRICS group of Brazil, Russia, India, China, and South Africa have been hit by the global slowdown and countries like India further singed by capital flow reversals. But this is a temporary phenomenon that will peter out sooner than later. *{It is true that growth rates of all BRICS countries have been declining because of global slowdown, and in India, capital (investment money) leaving; however, this phenomenon is only going to last for a short while, and the situation will turn around.}* BRICS economies are bound to reinvent the global economic order, and even fashion it in their own image, once the macroeconomic balances are restored and foreign investment flows rebound, boosted by reforms. *{The economies of BRICS countries will change the global structure and possibly redesign it once the situation turns around.}*

Similarly, the argument that the rest of the BRICS countries will fall by the wayside while China continues to march ahead is flawed. *{Also, it is not true that other BRICS countries will decline, but China will continue to progress.}* Not only has China's growth rate almost halved from peak levels, it's in fact facing a double whammy with its export-led economy badly hit by the slowdown in advanced country markets – as rising wages and a shortage of skills erode its competitive base even as it struggles to shift over to a domestic consumption-based growth model. *{China's growth rate is half of what it used to be, its export-based economy is slowed because of global slowdown, and its competitiveness is being damaged because wages are rising, but skills do not match.}* This will probably help other BRICS countries like India to make new inroads into the global markets for manufactured goods and close in fast on China. *{This negative situation for China will help India and other BRICS countries to enter and flourish in exports of manufactured goods and catch up to China's growth.}*

In fact, the most recent trends on the global Greenfield investments, which exclude mergers and acquisitions, validate this argument. *{Statistics also support this, especially data on global Greenfield investments (it is a type of Foreign Direct Investment [FDI] where an investor company not only invests money, but also opens facilities or offices in the country).}* The numbers show that while new FDI (Foreign Direct Investment) projects to China have come down sharply by almost half after the global slowdown, other BRICS countries haven't been so badly bruised. *{Such FDI investments have fallen sharply in China but not so badly in other countries.}* On the contrary, the gap between China and other BRICS countries has in fact shrunk, with India accounting for 30% of the Greenfield FDI projects into BRICS as compared to the 40% share of China. *{In fact, now the gap between India and China has reduced because India now has 30% of Greenfield Investments and China has 40%.}*

Main point: BRICS economies will rise again; the gap between other BRICS nations and China will become less.

Passage 2 (Dr. Walter, Professor, on BRICS countries)

Understanding the Passage

The economist's assessment that the BRICS era is at an end is right on the money. *{The dominating time of the BRICS nations is at the end.}* Despite witnessing robust economic growth in the last decade, each of the BRICS countries faces a unique set of problems today. *{After strong growth, now every BRICS nation has lot of problems.}* The recent global economic downturn has exposed structural infirmities that will prevent these economies from returning to a high growth trajectory anytime soon. *{The global slowdown has shown weaknesses in the economic structures of these countries, weaknesses which will prevent the countries from returning to high growth in the foreseeable future.}* Besides, neither is it realistic to expect these emerging markets to grow faster from a higher GDP base than their previous low threshold. *{Also, it is illogical to expect that these developing economies will grow faster now, because now they have higher GDP; earlier they had lower GDP, so their growth was higher.}*

In India, the economy is wracked by a rupee in free fall (by over 30%), high inflation (touching double digits) and a burgeoning current account deficit (almost 5% of GDP). *{India's situation is dire; its rupee is declining, inflation is high and the deficit between imports and exports is alarming.}* Recent months have seen significant capital outflows with foreign investors opting to park their funds in a recovering US economy. *{Given India's situation, capital flows are reversing and instead going to the US.}* The petering out of growth sentiments is directly related to the failure of the political leadership to affect a much-needed second wave of economic reforms. And with policy paralysis expected to sustain, the India growth story remains in limbo. *{The situation in India is so bad because of problems with the political scenario which did not bring about the necessary economic reforms; since this lack of reforms is supposed to remain, growth seems unlikely.}* In both Brazil and Russia, the weakening of commodity prices has hit the economies hard, exposing their over-reliance on natural resources as cash cows. *{In Brazil and Russia, the economies are strapped for cash because they depended too much on natural resources, but are now suffering since commodity prices have fallen.}* Meanwhile, South Africa's economy has been hurting since a recession that affected several crucial industries. *{SA's economy is in trouble because the recession has affected important industries.}* In China, the economy is transitioning from resource-intensive, investment-led growth to a consumption-oriented pattern. *{In China, the economy is changing from needing lots of resources to needing less, and from being investment-based to consumption-based.}* Add to this the massive global pressure to appreciate the yuan, and it is clear that China would need to affect a not-so-easy overhaul of its economic model to maintain high growth. *{Even China will need to restructure its economic model.}* However, as the economist points out, given China's planned economic model and ability to move resources without political missteps, it is best placed among the BRICS nations to pull out of the middle-income trap. *{However, it has the capability and therefore will pull out and progress.}* Taken together, the global heft that the BRICS bloc wielded is over. *{The dominating time of the BRICS nations is at an end.}* And while these emerging markets will continue to grow, they will need to get used to moderate rates of growth. *{These markets will grow but not at as fast a pace as they did.}*

Main Point: The BRICS economies will not return to their earlier growth; only China might. The era of BRICS economy is over.

Question 1-Solution

We have been asked to find aspects on which the authors of both passages will agree.

Let's analyze the options one by one.

(A)   This option is **correct.** Look at Passage A, lines 2-4, Mike says *No doubt the growth rates in the BRICS group of Brazil, Russia, India, China and South Africa have been hit by the global slowdown* and in line 5-7, *BRICS economies are bound to reinvent the global economic order and even fashion it in their own image* .

Look at Passage B, lines 2-4, Dr. Walter says *Despite witnessing robust economic growth in the last decade, each of the BRICS countries faces a unique set of problems today.*

We can infer that both agree that BRICS countries experienced good economic growth in the past.

(B)   This option is **incorrect.** Passage 1, line 5; *But this is a temporary phenomenon that will peter out **sooner** than later*- Mike opines that BRICS economies will bounce back soon. Passage 2, lines 3-5, *The recent global economic downturn has exposed structural infirmities that will **prevent these economies from returning to a high growth trajectory anytime soon.**-* The second commentator opines that BRICS economies will not be able to bounce back soon.

Both will disagree on the timeframe.

(C)   This option is **incorrect.** Passage 1, lines 14-15; *its (**China's**) competitive base even as it **struggles to shift** over to a **domestic consumption-based growth model.**-* The first commentator opines that it will be difficult for China to shift over to a consumption-based economy. Passage 2, paragraph 2, lines 17-18, *In China, the economy is **transitioning** from resource-intensive, investment-led growth to a **consumption-oriented** pattern-* The second commentator opines that the Chinese economy is on the course of transforming to a consumption-based economy.

Both will disagree on this aspect.

(D)   This option is **incorrect.** Passage 1, paragraph 3 – Mike expresses positivity towards the growth prospects of the Indian economy. Passage 2, paragraph 2 – Dr Walter expresses pessimism towards the growth prospects of the Indian economy, suggesting that unless the political scenario changes, growth will be in limbo.

Both will disagree on this aspect.

The correct answer is A.

Question 2-Solution

We have to find an option that cannot be inferred from the passages above. In other words, three options can be inferred but one cannot be.

Let's analyze the options one by one.

(A)   This option is **incorrect**. Refer to Passage 2, lines 14-16; *In both Brazil and Russia, the **weakening of commodity prices has hit the economies hard**, exposing their **over-reliance on natural resources** as cash cows.* We can infer that Brazil and Russia's economies are dependent on natural resources, option A can be inferred, but regarding the weakening of commodity prices, we can only infer that it has impacted Brazil and Russia hard, but not benefitted China–option C.

(B)   This option is **incorrect** because option B can also be inferred. Refer to Passage 2, lines 10-11; *Recent months have seen significant capital outflows with foreign investors **opting to park their funds in a recovering US economy**.*

(C)   This option is **correct** because as discussed in option A, option C does not have any support in either passage.

(D)   This option is **incorrect** because option D can also be inferred. Refer to Passage 1, lines 23-25; *On the contrary, the gap between China and other BRICS countries has in fact shrunk, with India accounting for 30% of the Greenfield FDI projects into BRICS as compared to the 40% share of China.* Among BRICS countries, only India is closest to China with 30% of the Greenfield FDI projects into BRICS, it means that other BRICS countries must account for much less than 40% of the Greenfield FDI projects into BRICS.

The correct answer is option C.

Question 3-Solution

This is a function question from the general category.

We have to find rhetorical devices (verbal tools of persuasion) that have been used by both passages.

Let's analyze the options one by one.

(A)   This option is **incorrect** because while the authors use observations, we cannot necessarily say that the observations cited in the passages are "personal" (made by the authors themselves).

(B)   This option is **incorrect** because no hypothetical situations have been used in the passage; such use would have been demonstrated by "if" sentences.

(C)   This option is **correct** because both the authors provide plenty of quantitative data to make various claims and support their points. In passage 1, quantitative data is present in the final paragraph, while in passage 2 it is present in the first few lines of the second paragraph.

(D)   This option is **incorrect** because neither author compares groups with any other group. Both authors are discussing only a single group (BRICS) and its members, but not comparing groups.

The correct answer is C.

Question 4 -Solution

This is a specific detail question.

We have been asked to find the opinion which is held only by the author of passage 2 about China but not by the author of passage 1. The opinion of the author of passage 2 about China can be found in the second half of the second paragraph: "*China would need to affect a not-so-easy overhaul of its economic model to maintain high growth*" and "*given China's planned economic model and ability to move resources without political missteps, it is best placed among the BRICS nations to pull out of the middle-income trap*". Thus, the author of passage 2 believes that China needs an overhaul of its economic model but also that its economy is going to grow the most from among the BRICS nations.

Let's analyze the options one by one.

(A) This option is **incorrect** because this is the opinion of the author of passage 1, who states that the gap between China and other BRICS nations is closing.

(B) This option is **correct** because this matches our deductions above.

(C) This option is **incorrect** because this is not given in the passage, and it is more likely to be the opinion of the author of passage 1, not of passage 2.

(D) This option is **incorrect** because this is not stated in the passage at all.

The correct answer is B.

Question 5-Solution

We have been asked to provide the best evidence for the opinion held only by the author of passage 2 about China. The opinion of the author of passage 2 about China can be found in the second half of the second paragraph: Lines 19-20 "*China would need to affect a not-so-easy overhaul of its economic model to maintain high growth*" and Lines 21-23 "*given China's planned economic model and ability to move resources without political missteps, it is best placed among the BRICS nations to pull out of the middle-income trap*". Thus, the author of passage 2 believes that China needs an overhaul of its economic model, but also that its economy is going to grow the most among the BRICS nations, using the above two sentences.

Let's analyze the options one by one.

(A) This option is **incorrect** because the sentence "*In India, the economy is wracked by a rupee in free fall (by over 30%), high inflation (touching double digits) and a burgeoning current account deficit (almost 5% of GDP)*" does not provide the author's opinion about China.

(B) This option is **correct** because the sentence "*However, as the economist points out, given China's planned economic model and ability to move resources without political missteps, it is best placed among the BRICS nations to pull out of the middle-income trap*" matches our deductions above.

(C) This option is **incorrect** because the sentence "*In China, the economy is transitioning from resource-intensive, investment-led growth to a consumption-oriented pattern*" is merely a fact provided by the author, but not his opinion.

(D) This option is **incorrect** because the sentence "*And while these emerging markets will continue to grow, they will need to get used to moderate rates of growth*" is too generic and does not contain the author's specific opinion about China.

The correct answer is B.

Question 6 -Solution

This is a specific Inference question from the general category.

We need to find the correct contrast between the views of the authors of each passage. We know that the author of passage 1 states that the gap between China and other BRICS nations is closing. The author of passage 2 states China's economy is going to grow the most among the BRICS nations.

Let's analyze the options one by one.

(A) This option is **incorrect** because while the option is correct about the author of passage 1, it is incorrect about the author of passage 2, who believes that China will grow, but other BRICS nations won't.

(B) This option is **incorrect** because the author of passage 1 does not suggest that only India will grow, but that BRICS nations will turn the negative situation around.

(C) This option is **correct** because this matches our deductions above.

(D) This option is **incorrect** because the author of passage 1 does not suggest that China will be overtaken by other BRICS nations, but rather that the gap between China and other nations is closing; also, the author of passage 2 does not state that China will get ahead of every other nation, but will be the only one from among BRICS nations to progress.

The correct answer is C.

Question 7 -Solution

This is a tone question.

We have been asked to find a pair of countries about which the author of passage 2 has a positive and negative opinion about growth prospects respectively, that is, the author should be positive towards the growth prospects of the first country and negative towards the growth prospects of the second. The author of passage 2 feels that China is the only country with the possibility of turning around the negative situation, while he feels that the other countries, i.e. India, Brazil, Russia, and South Africa, are unlikely to make any significant progress.

Let's analyze the options one by one.

(A) This option is **correct** because this matches our deductions above.

(B)   This option is **incorrect** because the author does not feel positive about India and negative about China; if this option were "China and India", it would have been correct.

(C)   This option is **incorrect** because the author does not feel positive about India but does feel negative about Brazil.

(D)   This option is **incorrect** because even though the author feels positive about China, he does not feel negative about the situation of the US.

The correct answer is A.

Question 8 -Solution

We have been asked to find a statement about India with which both the authors will agree. The author of passage 1 feels that India's growth prospects are good despite facing a global slowdown and capital flow reversals. The author of passage 2 feels that India's growth prospects are not good because of a bad political situation and "significant capital outflows" (line 10). Thus, both the authors would only agree about the capital flow reversals.

Let's analyze the options one by one.

(A)   This option is **incorrect** because only the author of passage 2 will agree with this option, but not the author of passage 1.

(B)   This option is **correct** because this matches our deductions above.

(C)   This option is **incorrect** because the author of passage 2 will not agree with this option, but the author of passage 1 will.

(D)   This option is **incorrect** because only the author of passage 2 will agree with this option, but not the author of passage 1.

The correct answer is B.

Question 9 -Solution

We have been asked to find the meaning of the phrase "peter out".
Let's analyze the sentences and examine the phrase "peter out".
"But this is a temporary phenomenon that will peter out sooner than later. BRICS economies are bound to reinvent the global economic order" – The sentences mean that some phenomenon of slowdown in BRICS is going to "peter out", and the BRICS are bound to grow. Thus, "peter out" must mean slowly diminish.
Even in the second passage, the meaning seems to remain the same.
"The petering out of growth sentiments is directly related to the failure of the political leadership to affect a much-needed second wave of economic reforms" – This sentence comes right after the sentence that states that capital flows have been reversed, thus growth sentiments have "petered out", or "diminished".
Let's analyze the options one by one.

(A)   This option is **incorrect** because "vanish" means "disappear without a trace"; it is too extreme to mean "reduce slowly, or diminish".

(B) This option is **incorrect** because "mushroom" means "grow"; it is the opposite of what is needed.

(C) This option is **correct** because this matches our deductions above; "abate" means "diminish/lessen".

(D) This option is **incorrect** because "exacerbate" means "worsen", but not necessarily "reduce/diminish".

The correct answer is C.

Chart for questions # 10 & 11

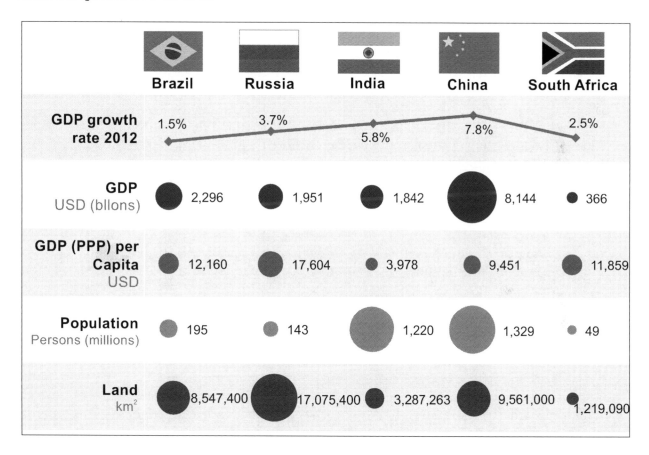

Question 10 -Solution

We have to deduce which of the following statements is supported by the graph.

Let us analyze each option one by one.

(A) This is **incorrect** because though the country that has the highest GDP is China ($8,144 B), and it also has the largest population (1,329 M), GDP per Capita income is highest ($17,604) for Russia, not China.

(B) This is **incorrect** because the country with the largest land is Russia (17,075,400 sq. km), and it also has the highest GDP per Capita income ($17,604). So Russia has one more parameter that is the highest among all countries.

(C)   This is **correct** because the country with the lowest population is South Africa (49 M), and it does not have the largest or the highest value for any of the remaining four parameters.

(D)   This is **incorrect** because the country with the highest GDP growth rate is China (7.8%), but among the other four parameters, it only has the highest GDP ($8,144), and population (1329 M) – only two parameters, and not at least three.

The correct answer is C.

Question 11 -Solution

The question wants us to calculate the ratio of land to population for each of the given four countries – Brazil, Russia, India, and China; it is to be noted that South Africa is not among them.

The traditional approach would be to calculate the ratios four times and reach the answer, however it is not required.

For the ratio $\frac{\text{land}}{\text{population}}$ to be the largest , we need the country that has the largest land and the lowest population, and that would be the answer. Its numerator (here, land) must be the largest, and its denominator (here, population) must be the smallest.

We see that the measurement of land is the highest for Russia, and its population is lowest, thus we have the desired country – Russia– for the correct answer.

What if the measurement of land had been the highest for Russia, but the population had been the lowest for some other country? Well, in that case, you might have to calculate ratios for at least a couple of countries.

If, for instance, South Africa were also there among the countries, then the questions might require some calculation. Still, not really; a logical deduction can sort out this, too.

In this alternate scenario, now the measurement of land is highest for Russia and the population is lowest for South Africa, so we must analyze the situation. We see that South Africa's population is almost $1/3 = 49/143$ of that of Russia, whereas Russia's land is more than 14 (17,075,400/1,219,090) times that of South Africa, thus the ratio of $\frac{\text{land}}{\text{population}}$ would still be higher for Russia. For your ready reference, $\frac{\text{land}}{\text{population}}$ for Russia = 119,408, and $\frac{\text{land}}{\text{population}}$ for South Africa = 24,879.

The correct answer is B.

7.11   Passage 11: Paired passage (Biographies on Hemingway)

Passage 1 (Dillon-Malone's biography on Hemingway)

Understanding the Passage

Nowhere in his derivative biography does Aubrey Dillon-Malone explain why he felt the world needed another Hemingway biography. *{The author feels that Dillon-Mallone's biography is pointless, that there was no need for another Hemingway biography; there is enough work on Hemingway.}* A Dublin-based novelist, Dillon-Malone seems to have stumbled upon his subject in the same way that Michael Palin did: through a fascination with Hemingway's singular form of American celebrity. *{The author believes that Dillon-Mallone(D-M) wrote this biography only because he was fascinated by Hemingway's odd, deep, and abiding fame; this same fascination also led Michael Palin to write a book on Hemingway.}*Indeed, the recurring focus on Hemingway's "Americaness" is the only element of this work that distinguishes it from Kurt Singer's and Milt Machlin's biographies. *{This focus on Hemingway's "American nature" is the only point of distinction between D-M's work and biographies by Singer and Machlin; thus, everything else is in these books, probably because D-M has "borrowed" material from Singer and Machlin.}*Those works were dubbed by Philip Young "vulture biographies," and Dillon-Malone's biography, like those by Singer and Machlin, feeds without attribution from earlier, careful work by serious Hemingway biographers. *{Such type of copied, unoriginal works have been termed "vulture biographies" by Philip Young; such biographies copy material from other serious and more dedicated biographies without properly giving credit or references.}*By sloppily blending the all too familiar facts of Hemingway's life with the equally familiar echoes in his fiction, Dillon-Malone has generated 358 pages of prose that only occasionally generate glimmers of interest for the reader. *{Dillon-Mallone's biography of 358 pages contains nothing new – familiar facts and familiar discussions on works of Hemingway blended in a careless, untidy manner.}*Dillon-Malone's goal is to lay down the "facts" of Hemingway's life to pierce the bubble of the "Hemingway legend." *{D-M's biography intends to present the so-called facts of Hemingway's life, to unveil the mystery behind Hemingway's fame and reputation.}*Many sentences are organized around phrases such as "the truth of the incident" or "the reality of the situation." *{D-M liberally uses sentences to present his opinion but dresses them as though they are real, verified facts.}* This absence of nuance may engage readers who are tired of scanning footnotes and deciphering carefully reasoned opinions, yet the unearned authoritative biographical voice of Dillon-Malone is difficult to trust even on simple matters. *{D-M's lack of appreciation for the finer differences leaves intelligent readers out and will interest only those readers who do not want careful, thorough opinions.}* Paradoxically, Dillon-Malone celebrates the same values he critiques. As Hemingway scholarship has moved far beyond the confines of this "legendary image," Dillon-Malone's interpretation is not especially refreshing or enlightening. *{Strangely, D-M praises the same values that he criticizes in Hemingway. D-M's approach and text is full of clichés and nothing new.}* Perhaps the only thing to be learned from this biography is Dillon-Malone's opinion of Hemingway. His impressions are decisive, judgmental, and predictable. According to Dillon-Malone, Hemingway was an uneven writer, and a disappointment as a human being. There is very little thoughtful commentary here on Hemingway's fiction. *{The only information one can get from D-M's book is D-M's opinions, which are sharp and judgmental, but not new. D-M suggests that Hemingway was not a particularly good person, and not a great writer. D-M does not provide any layered analysis on Hemingway's work.}* In sum, even as a celebrity biography aiming to entertain a mass-market audience, *Hemingway: The Grace and the Pressure* misses its mark. *{D-M's book does not live up to any standards.}* Derivative, repetitive, and poorly organized, the book manages to make a dramatic life dull. *{The book is unoriginal, repetitive, and not structured well.}*Divorces, plane crashes, fistfights, and war wounds are recounted in a style that is crude and heavy-handed. *{It lacks proper, sensible treatment of the incidents of Hemingway's life.}* Dillon-Malone has done no original research, and all of the twenty-four black and white photos are overly familiar. Dillon-Malone's biography only deserves a place on the lowest bookshelf beside the works of Milt Machlin, Kurt Singer, and Peter Buckley. *{It only deserves to be ranked lowest of the low.}*

Main point: Dillon-Mallone's book is unnecessary, below par, and ill-constructed.

Passage 2 (Wagner-Martin's biography on Hemingway)

Understanding the Passage

Unlike his contemporaries Fitzgerald and Steinbeck, Ernest Hemingway managed to maintain a literary dominance that continued steadily during his life and has wavered only slightly in the years since his death in 1961. *{Hemingway has remained an important literary figure many decades after his death, unlike his contemporaries Fitzgerald and Steinbeck.}* Linda Wagner-Martin's "*Earnest Hemingway*" constitutes an indispensable source for general readers and scholars alike as we enter the new century. *{Wagner-Martin's book is a necessary source of information for both scholars and general readers.}* As Wagner-Martin notes in her introduction, Hemingway–although an "incurable romantic"–was remarkable for the serious way in which he addressed the business of writing. In addition to his unique, economic style and his portraits of life that shocked and intrigued many of his early readers, he influenced the entire genre of "hard-boiled" mystery and detective fiction. *{Hemingway is a romantic in his writing style, which cannot be changed but he is also very serious about his writing and views it in a systematic way (discussed by Wagner-Martin(W-M) in her book). Hemingway had a tight writing style, using minimum and precise writing, and he wrote characters that were shocking. In addition, he had a strong impact regarding the creation of the genre of mystery and detective writing.}* Through his writing as well as his public persona, his pursuit and successful achievement of the American dream positions him as an engaging subject for a historically focused examination, for Hemingway metaphorically represents and reflects the issues that preoccupied Americans of his era: issues of world war, of gender, of industry and ecology, of human triumph and loss. *{Hemingway has remained popular even now because he successfully achieved the American dream and dealt with issues that were important to his generation, issues such as world war, gender, industry, ecology, human values, etc. Such details about Hemingway became available through his writing and his public image.}* One theoretical method that has recently benefited Hemingway scholarship is intertextuality, the borrowing of or references to other fictional works. *{A recent method of studying Hemingway has come to light –intertextuality, which means writing something while referring to some other writer or his work.}* Wagner-Martin identifies numerous ways in which Hemingway responds to the fiction and the writers of his time. *{ W-M's book shows many instances where Hemingway used this.}* Indeed, so deeply was Hemingway immersed in literature of both the 19th and the 20th century that, in adapting those works to his own art, he became a pioneer in the technique of intertextuality. *{Hemingway completely mastered the art of intertextuality.}* Citing a number of writers and novels that influenced Hemingway, Wagner-Martin discusses in particular Hemingway's extensive use of Henry James and she draws several significant conclusions about the ways in which Hemingway wanted readers to see that he was different from–and, he doubtless hoped, better than–these older masters. After all, he actually told Charles Scribner that he wanted to "beat dead writers" that he considered first-rate artists. *{W-M's book cites numerous such intertextual instances. Hemingway wanted readers to compare his writing with that of other great writers, and he wanted to emerge triumphant, as proven by his quote.}*

This superb handbook for understanding Hemingway in our own time is followed by an extremely useful illustrated chronology that parallels events in Hemingway's own life with concurrent historical events and publication dates of other significant literature. *{W-M's book is important, specifically for the modern time. It provides a detailed chronology of events that show important events alongside events from Hemingway's life.}* Wagner-Martin's book is an invaluable tool to both the general reader and the Hemingway scholar: indeed, ignoring this book would render much of Hemingway disappointingly inaccessible to the contemporary reader. *{W-M's book is a necessary source of information for both scholars and general readers. Without it, readers will not have access to Hemingway.}*

Main point: Wagner-Martin's book is necessary to understand Hemingway in contemporary times.

Question 1-Solution

This is a main purpose question from the general category.

We have been asked to find the subject of the primary discussion of the authors. The author of passage 1 is discussing a biography of Hemingway by Dillon-Mallone, while the author of passage 2 is discussing a biography of Hemingway by Wagner-Martin. Thus, both the passages are discussing biographies on Hemingway.

Let's analyze the options one by one.

(A)   This option is **incorrect** because while the authors discuss Hemingway's life in discussing Hemingway's biographies, they do so in passing; this is not their primary discussion.

(B)   This option is **incorrect** because the authors do not discuss Hemingway's works, but rather works on Hemingway as their primary discussion.

(C)   This option is **correct** because this matches our deductions above.

(D)   This option is **incorrect** because this is discussed briefly, not as a primary discussion.

The correct answer is C.

Question 2-Solution

This is a function question from the general category.

We have to find some rhetorical device that passage 2 does not have, but passage 1 does. Passage 1 uses comparisons; Dillon-Mallone's work is compared with other biographies. Such comparison of the primary work in discussion with other similar works is not present in passage 2. Passage 1 uses personal opinions about the biography, just as passage 2 does. Thus, option D is incorrect. Similarly, both passages present a detailed critique of the biographies. Option C is also incorrect. Only passage 2 provides actual quotes and references from various sources to support its case, but passage 1 does not.

Thus, the correct answer is A.

Question 3-Solution

This is an inference question.

We have been asked to find the opinion on Hemingway of the author of passage 1. While the author does not directly present his opinion on Hemingway, it can be inferred from his opinions of Dillon-Mallone's comments on Hemingway. Dillon-Mallone suggests that Hemingway was an uneven writer, and was disappointing as a human being. The author thoroughly disagrees with Dillon-Mallone, and thus is likely to believe that Hemingway was a consistent writer and not a disappointing human being. Also, the author states that Dillon-Mallone makes Hemingway's dramatic life sound dull. Thus, the author also believes that Hemingway had an interesting, dramatic life.

Let's analyze the options one by one.

(A)   This option is **correct** because this matches our deductions above.

(B)   This option is **incorrect** because this is Dillon-Mallone's opinion, and the opposite of what the author is likely to believe.

(C)   This option is **incorrect** because this is the opposite of what the author is likely to believe.

(D)   This option is **incorrect** because this is Dillon-Mallone's opinion, and the opposite of what the author is likely to believe.

The correct answer is A.

Question 4 -Solution

This is a tone question.

We have been asked which book would be important for a person trying to understand Hemingway's works, as can be understood from the two passages. Thus, we need to find out which book on Hemingway has been positively received by the authors. We know that the author of passage 1 finds Dillon-Mallone's book (Hemingway: the Grace and the Pressure) completely below par, and equates it to books by Peter Buckley and Milt Machlin. Thus, those books would not be recommended by the author. We also know that the author of passage 2 finds Wagner-Martin's book (Earnest Hemingway) indispensable (necessary) and is thus likely to recommend that book.

Let's analyze the options one by one.

(A)   This option is **incorrect** because this is Dillon-Mallone's book, which the author finds substandard.

(B)   This option is **correct** because this matches our deductions above.

(C)   This option is **incorrect** because the author equates Dillon-Mallone's book, which he finds substandard, with Peter Buckley's book.

(D)   This option is **incorrect** because the author only mentions Michael Palin's book in passing, in discussing the reason for Dillon-Mallone writing the biography; however, what he feels about Palin's book cannot be gauged from the passage.

The correct answer is B.

Question 5-Solution

This is a function question from the general category.

We have to find some rhetorical device that passage 1 does not have, but passage 2 does. Passage 1 uses comparisons; Dillon-Mallone's work is compared with other biographies. Such comparison of the primary work in discussion with other similar works is not present in passage 2. Passage 1 uses personal opinions about the biography, just as passage 2 does. Both passages present a detailed evaluation and analysis of the biographies. Only passage 2 provides actual quotes and references from various sources to support its cases, i.e. attributions to make its points.

Thus, the correct answer is B.

Question 6 -Solution

This is a detail question.

We have to find the reason that the author believes Dillon-Malone wrote a biography on Hemingway. This can be found in the first few lines of the passage itself: "*Dillon-Malone seems to have stumbled upon his subject in the same way that Michael Palin did: through a fascination with Hemingway's singular form of American celebrity.*"

Thus, the author feels that Dillon-Mallon wrote a biography on Hemingway because he was fascinated by Hemingway's fame and reputation.

Let's analyze the options one by one.

(A)   This option is **correct** because this matches our deductions above.

(B)   This option is **incorrect** because this is not stated in the passage, nor is it implied by the author.

(C)   This option is **incorrect** because Dillon-Mallone actually believed Hemingway to be an uneven writer, not a good one.

(D)   This option is **incorrect** because the author suggests that there was plenty of work on Hemingway already, leaving now the question of the author assuming that DM would have later written a biography for lack of one on Hemingway.

The correct answer is A.

Question 7 -Solution

This is a detail question.

The question asks us the reasons for the importance of Wagner-Martin's book. The reasons are cited by the author in the final paragraph, in which the author states that the book is necessary for scholars and readers, especially in our time. Thus, the author suggests that the book provides proper perspective for contemporary readers and scholars.

Let's analyze the options one by one.

(A)   This option is **incorrect** because this is out of the scope of passage 2.

(B)   This option is **correct** because this matches our deductions above.

(C)   This option is **incorrect** because the author does not state that intertextuality was not discussed by any other work; the author only states that Wagner-Martin's book goes into detail on it.

(D)   This option is **incorrect** because this is too generic, and not the reason cited by the author for recommending Wagner-Martin's book.

The correct answer is B.

Question 8 -Solution

This is a tone question.

We have been asked to find the relationship between the first and the second passages in their verdict on the biographies they critique. We know that passage 1 is extremely negative about the work it discusses, while passage 2 is appreciative.

Let's analyze the options one by one.

(A)   This option is **incorrect** because the author of passage 1 does not endorse (approve of) the work; he criticizes it sharply.

(B)   This option is **incorrect** because the author of passage 1 does not even cautiously appreciate the work; he criticizes it sharply.

(C)   This option is **incorrect** because the author of passage 2 does not remain neutral about the work in discussion; he praises it extensively.

(D)   This option is **correct** because this matches our deductions above.

The correct answer is D.

Question 9 -Solution

We have been asked to find lines that provide evidence to explain **why** Hemingway was so persistently famous among all.

Let's analyze the options one by one.

(A)   This option is **incorrect** because the sentence *"Unlike his contemporaries Fitzgerald and Steinbeck, Ernest Hemingway managed to maintain a literary dominance that continued steadily during his life and has wavered only slightly in the years since his death in 1961"* does not explain **why** Hemingway was so persistently famous but merely states that he was.

(B)   This option is **incorrect** because the sentence *"Linda Wagner-Martin's "Earnest Hemingway" constitutes an indispensable source for general readers and scholars alike as we enter the new century"* only discusses Wagner-Martin's book and its value, but not why Hemingway was popular.

(C)   This option is **correct** because the sentence *"Through his writing as well as his public persona, his pursuit and successful achievement of the American dream positions him as an engaging subject for a historically focused examination, for Hemingway metaphorically represents and reflects the issues that preoccupied Americans of his era: issues of world war, of gender, of industry and ecology, of human triumph and loss"* explains exactly **why** Hemingway was so famous, and what constituted his appeal.

(D)   This option is **incorrect** because the sentence *"A Dublin-based novelist, Dillon-Malone seems to have stumbled upon his subject in the same way that Michael Palin did: through a fascination with Hemingway's singular form of American celebrity"* does not explain **why** Hemingway was so persistently famous, but merely states that he was.

The correct answer is C.

Question 10 -Solution

This is an inference question.

We have been asked to find Hemingway's beliefs from the information given in the passages.

Let's analyze the options one by one.

(A)   This option is **correct** because this can be inferred from the third paragraph of the second passage, in which the author quotes Hemingway as wanting to refer (through intertextuality) to old, masterful, great writers in order to "beat" them. Also, the passage mentions that Hemingway refers to Henry James quite a lot, thus implying that Hemingway must have believed James to be a great writer whom he wanted to "beat".

(B)   This option is **incorrect** because this cannot be inferred from the passage.

(C)   This option is **incorrect** because we cannot necessarily infer this from the passage; the passage only mentions that Hemingway's dominance continued more than Fitzgerald's or Steinbeck's.

(D) This option is **incorrect** because why Hemingway reflected on the issues he did is not discussed.

The correct answer is A.

Chapter 8

Talk to Us

Have a Question?

Email your questions to info@manhattanreview.com. We will be happy to answer you. Your questions can be related to a concept, an application of a concept, an explanation of a question, a suggestion for an alternate approach, or anything else you wish to ask regarding the SAT.

Do mention the page number when quoting from the book.

Best of luck!

Professor Dr. Joern Meissner
& The Manhattan Review Team

Manhattan Admissions

**You are a unique candidate with unique experience.
We help you to sell your story to the admissions committee.**

Manhattan Admissions is an educational consulting firm that guides academic candidates through the complex process of applying to the world's top educational programs. We work with applicants from around the world to ensure that they represent their personal advantages and strength well and get our clients admitted to the world's best business schools, graduate programs and colleges.

We will guide you through the whole admissions process:

- ✓ **Personal Assessment and School Selection**
- ✓ **Definition of your Application Strategy**
- ✓ **Help in Structuring your Application Essays**
- ✓ **Unlimited Rounds of Improvement**
- ✓ **Letter of Recommendation Advice**
- ✓ **Interview Preparation and Mock Sessions**
- ✓ **Scholarship Consulting**

To schedule a free 30-minute consulting and candidacy evaluation session or read more about our services, please visit or call:

 www.manhattanadmissions.com   **+1.212.334.2500**

Made in United States
Orlando, FL
29 August 2022

21704425R00111